THE MATRIX: UNLOCKED

First published 2003 by **Contender Books**
Contender Books is a division of
The Contender Entertainment Group
48 Margaret Street
London
W1W 8SE

This edition published 2003

1 3 5 7 9 10 8 6 4 2

ISBN 1 84357 093 9

Printed in the UK by **Butler & Tanner Ltd**, Frome and London
Cover design and typesetting by **Craig Stevens** at **Designsection**
Edited by **Jacqueline Rayner/Ian Atkins**
Production by **Sasha Morton**

THE MATRIX: UNLOCKED

AN UNAUTHORISED REVIEW OF THE MATRIX PHENOMENON

PAUL CONDON

ACKNOWLEDGEMENTS

This book is dedicated to Ian, Lisa and Joshua

- To my Mum and Dad – just because you're both The One to me.
- To everyone in my fantastic family – godparents San and Kev; the cousins I spent many happy summers with, Neil, Rachael, Graeme, Yvonne and Bernie. Love you all heaps.
- And of course to the Ormskirk Mafia – Joan, Dot, Jim and Babs – I don't get to see you as often as I'd like, for which I can only apologise.
- To my fantastic friends, who are there for me whenever I need them to be – to Bob, Steve, Jules, and everyone back up in the old LSCT catchment area... hope you appreciate the DW twaddle!
- To Wendy, Lesley and everyone at the Retro, the friendliest place in London (mine's a vodka and coke). And now this book's finished, tell Kevin I'll be back for karaoke...
- To everyone on the 6th Floor – bless you for putting up with my boring stories and for making allowances for this darned book. Major thanks especially to Richard, Lea, Joe, Ian, Jo L, Richard and Sam. I'm back to full strength now, promise!
- Everyone else in work who's been supportive – especially Kate, Athena, Jo B, the DNA-ers, Esther, Amani, the IPs, Dan D (for the valuable links!) and Nelly. All of you make my day.
- To the wonderful inanity of the klakking posse. Not to mention Andrew Hub...
- To the people behind the NP2CD. I wish I'd been able to hear it earlier!
- And to my holiday chums: GR, JB, JH, DH, JH and the glittery LB. Roll on September!
- To the fantastic team at Contender, particularly Sasha, Michèle, Kate and Jac. Your patience was much appreciated!
- Finally, and most importantly, to my flatmate Jim for all of his help with research on this book – couldn't have done it without ya, matey.

INTRODUCTION

It is a truth universally acknowledged that most science-fiction fans are not what you'd describe as 'cool'. From the stereotypical 'anorak' to the Comic Book Store owner in *The Simpsons*, followers of science fiction, horror and fantasy media have largely been portrayed as objects of pity, or at best, with a touch of ridicule. When Warner Bros released a science-fiction movie in 1999, few people could have predicted the impact that it would have around the globe. For a start, there wasn't a huge amount of advance publicity – all of the world's media were much more interested in previewing the long awaited prequel to the *Star Wars* saga, *The Phantom Menace*. Furthermore, the directors of this movie didn't exactly have a stellar track record, with only one other feature film under their belts. And perhaps the biggest liability to the success of this movie was the fact that the star of the film was an actor who was held in fairly low esteem by practically every critic across the globe.

And yet, *The Matrix* was a staggering success.

Rarely in recent times has a movie grabbed the public consciousness in the way *The Matrix* has. From the moment that the first film was released, the cult of *The Matrix* began to grow and spread like some kind of disease. People started going back to the cinema to see the film for a second, third, even fourth time. When it was released on sell-through format, it became the first DVD to find its way into many people's homes. *The Matrix* was a film that actually rewarded repeated viewing – unlike most movies, the more times you watched it, the more you got out of it. Because the action and special-effects sequences were so outstanding, so cutting edge, it was a joy to watch them time and again – particularly when it became possible to re-watch all of the 'cool' bits in the privacy of your own home. And perhaps more importantly, each time you saw *The Matrix*, another nuance of the plot became clearer. You saw yet another visual trick or in-joke that reinforced the themes and storyline. Eventually, you became a disciple of *The Matrix*, a follower of The One yourself. At last, it was cool to be a sci-fi geek.

So that, hopefully, is where this book comes in. *The Matrix* and its sequels are an ever-expanding universe of references, ideas, concepts and really tight-fitting PVC outfits. It's in tribute to the coolest universe in science fiction and the genius brothers behind that universe that this book has been written.

This book covers the world of *The Matrix* as detailed in the movies *The Matrix* and *The Matrix: Reloaded*, in the animated shorts of *The Animatrix*, and via the computer game *Enter The Matrix*. At the time of writing, there are still five months to go until the worldwide release of *The Matrix: Revolutions*, and as yet very little of the plotline has leaked out. Perhaps this is quite apt. After all, these films are essentially about how computerised information is controlled and restricted – it would be somehow disappointing if the current vogue for internet spoilers and rumours managed to ruin everyone's enjoyment of the final movie.

Before we begin, let's get one thing straight right now. This book has got nothing to do with Warner Bros, Village Roadshow Pictures, Silver Pictures or NPV Entertainment. This is a completely unauthorised book, which means that as the author I've got no secret access into the mind of the Wachowski Brothers. All of the contents of this book are therefore my own theories, my own interpretations and could consequently be completely wide of the mark. Despite this warning, I do hope that you'll carry on reading this book, simply because there's lots of interesting things I've been thinking about and I'd really like you to know about them too.

In order to get these fascinating facts about *The Matrix* films across in the simplest possible way, readers of this book are offered a choice: either take the Blue Pill or take the Red Pill.

Blue PilL

By taking the Blue Pill, you'll read about the fiction of *The Matrix*. This section is broken up into the following:

| What Is *The Matrix*? |

The full story of everything that happens to our heroes in *The Matrix* and *The Matrix: Reloaded*. The key events, the important quotes and the best action sequences are detailed here, primarily as a reminder of the events and how they unfolded.

| What Do You Do? |

The three main characters in *The Matrix* films are of course Neo, Trinity and Morpheus. The way in which those characters grow and evolve is one of the crowning achievements of the Wachowski Brothers, setting their film way above the simple shoot-'em-ups and all-action spectacles that tend to be the stock response from most science-fiction filmmakers.

| What's In A Name? |

One of the most common areas of discussion and debate amongst *Matrix* fans is the importance of the names chosen by the Wachowski Brothers for their characters. Discover how myth, legend, religion and historical characters provided inspiration – and potentially how these names may act as plot spoilers for *The Matrix: Revolutions*...

| Where Do You Come From? |

Providing a beginner's guide to the philosophical arguments and theories that are featured in *The Matrix* films, and the way in which modern philosophers have used these movies to further their own interpretations of life, the universe and everything.

| What Do You Believe? |

Most people watching *The Matrix* films are aware that many different religions are referenced, and this chapter features background on the major beliefs that the Wachowski Brothers tapped into for their films. So if you skipped your Religious Education classes at school and want to know more about how Buddhism influences the story of *The Matrix*, then this chapter is for you.

RED PILL

By taking the Red Pill, you will emerge out of the fictional world of *The Matrix* and into the reality of the movie-making industry. Contained in this section of the book are the following chapters:

| What Is *The Matrix*? |

A lightning-fast, subliminal journey through the raw data at the heart of *The Matrix* franchise. In this chapter you'll read about the filthy lucre, the locations used in making the films, plus some surprising behind-the-scenes facts. Just don't blink or you'll miss something really important!

| Who Are You? |

Ever spent time scratching your head, trying to remember exactly where you've seen somebody before? This chapter helps the inquisitive among you work out who did what, when, and in what films. It's a movie nerd's guide to where you can catch your favourite *Matrix* stars in their previous roles.

| Where Does *The Matrix* Come From? |

Although we all know that *The Matrix* movies are some of the most entertaining films made in the past few years, there are certain elements of the plotlines, themes and style of *The Matrix* that seem a little... well... familiar. In this chapter you can discover some of the films and books that the Wachowskis have acknowledged as being an influence on their movies, as well as some other TV shows and films that told similar stories many years ago.

| Deconstructing *The Matrix* |

We know that *The Matrix* is an extremely cool movie franchise, but why is that? How have the Men In Suits used a tale of rebellion and fighting back against the faceless powers of authority to boost their corporate coffers? By buying into *The Matrix*, are you yourself falling under the spell of the twenty-first century's very own hidden Matrix? And is it possible to predict what the contents of *The Matrix: Revolutions* might be, simply by looking at how Hollywood Movies always must be?

AppendiceS

Listing the cast and crew of both films (it's important to give credit where credit's due, don't you agree?), outlining the expansion to *The Matrix* universe seen in the nine *Animatrix* short films, and providing extra snippets of information on the clips of other movies and TV shows that are seen within the narrative of the movies.

Remember that unlike Neo, you do have the option of taking both the Blue Pill *and* the Red Pill – such are the advantages of paper over an ingestible locator program. Indeed, you can read the chapters of this book in any order. So if you're ready, plug yourself in, get out your copy of *The Matrix* soundtrack album, and let's crack on with uploading all that information.

Paul Condon

July 2003

BLUE PILL

100
100
100
001
000
101
010
100
110
100
001
100
100
101
000
010
100
001
011
000
010
110
101
000
101
011
101
001
001
010
101
010
101
001
001
011
001
001
000
010
001
010
101
001
101
000

100
100
100
001
000
101
010
100
110
100
001
100
100
101
000
010
100
001
011
000
010
110
101
000
101
011
101
001
001
010
101
010
101
001
001
011
001
001
000
010
001
010
101
001
101
000

So you've decided to take the Blue Pill? Well I can hardly blame you. The fantasy world that you're living in is a comfy place to stay. You're happy just knowing about things you're already familiar with, aren't you? You don't really like to step outside of your comfort zone. Well if you really don't want to take the Red Pill, I can't force you. Just make sure that you've examined all there is to find out about this fantasy world you're stuck inside. Then perhaps you'll be ready to discover what has really been going on underneath the surface...

What is the matrix?

| The Matrix |

A man and a woman have a terse conversation via telephone. It seems that they are hoping to discover if a person is 'The One', as someone called Morpheus believes. The man asks the woman if she believes that the person they are talking about is 'The One', but she doesn't confirm either yes or no. Just then, the woman realises that the line they are talking on might be tapped and quickly hangs up.

In a dilapidated city-centre hotel ('The Heart o' the City'), a group of armed police kicks in the door of room 303. Inside is a solitary woman, clad all in black. The police move forward, intent on handcuffing the woman, who stands still, apparently accepting her fate. At that moment, a car pulls up outside the hotel and three men dressed in smart suits and wearing sunglasses (even though it is night-time) climb out of the car. Their leader, Agent Smith, coolly tells the police lieutenant that his men are already dead...

The woman moves faster than is physically possible, disarming one officer, shooting another with his colleague's gun, running up and around the walls of the room in order to take the cops out. With all of the police subdued, the woman picks up a mobile phone and makes a call. She speaks to Morpheus, telling him that the line must have been traced. Morpheus confirms that the hard-line has been cut by 'them' and tells the woman, Trinity, that she must find another exit somewhere. Morpheus tells Trinity to focus – there are Agents closing in on her. As Trinity leaves the hotel room she sees an Agent and a group of policemen leaving the lift. Trinity runs for her life, trying to escape across the rooftops of nearby buildings. She leaps huge chasms between the buildings – distances seemingly impossible for a normal human to cover. Although the police are unable to follow, she is relentlessly pursued by one of the Agents, who matches, or even surpasses, her athleticism.

Trinity manages to evade the Agent and heads towards a phone booth situated on a street corner. As she approaches, she sees a huge refuse truck revving its engine, an Agent at the steering wheel. The phone rings – Trinity runs as fast as she can and picks up the telephone receiver, just as the truck smashes into the phone booth, demolishing it into rubble. The Agent is joined by his two colleagues. They appear unconcerned that Trinity seems to have escaped – indeed, there is no body in the wreckage of the phone booth. Instead they are delighted that the information they got from their informant appears to be real. Now they have the name of the next target – Neo.

Meanwhile, across the city, a young man has nodded off in front of his computer keyboard. Images of newspaper articles about Morpheus disappear from his monitor to be replaced by a plain green text message. 'Wake up, Neo…', the message reads. 'The Matrix has you.' The man, Thomas Anderson, stirs from his sleep and reads the message. The message on the computer screen tells him to 'Follow the white rabbit'. Just then, there's a knock at the door of his apartment. It's a group of techno-hackers, led by Choi and Dujour. Thomas tells them that they are two hours late for their appointment. Choi hands over $2000 to Thomas, who goes back into his apartment and gets a computer disk for them. Thomas warns Choi not to get caught using the disk. Choi comments that

Thomas looks whiter than usual – he advises Thomas that he needs some rest, that he 'needs to unplug'. Choi and Dujour invite Thomas to join them for a night out. He's about to refuse when he sees a tattoo of a white rabbit on Dujour's shoulder. Thomas changes his mind and joins them in a techno nightclub.

In the club, Thomas is approached by Trinity, who introduces herself and calls him by his hacker name, Neo. Thomas has heard of Trinity, who is a notorious computer hacker responsible for breaking into some major government computer records, but he's surprised – he'd always assumed that Trinity would be a man. Trinity tells him that she knows who Thomas is looking for, and that the real thing that Thomas is looking for isn't a person, but the answer to a question. Thomas knows what that question is – 'What is the Matrix?' Trinity tells Thomas that he's in danger, and that 'they' are watching him.

The next morning, Thomas wakes up late for his day job at the Metacortex Corporation. His boss, Mr Rhineheart, gives him a severe telling off, threatening him with dismissal if he doesn't get into work on time. Back at his desk, Thomas gets a package delivered to him. He opens it and discovers a mobile phone, which rings immediately. On the other end is Morpheus. He tells Thomas that he doesn't know if he is ready to see what he has to show him, but unfortunately they have both run out of time. At that moment, a group of Agents and police arrives in Thomas's office. Thomas tries to escape, with Morpheus giving him directions – almost as if he's watching everything that happens on a monitor somewhere. Cornered by the Agents, Thomas makes a last attempt to escape by climbing along a window ledge on to a window-cleaner's cradle. However Thomas's nerve gives out and he is arrested by the Agents. Trinity observes as Thomas is led away in a police car.

In custody later, Thomas is interrogated by Agent Smith. Smith offers Thomas a deal. Although they have a huge file on the crimes he has committed under his hacker alias, Neo, they will put them all aside if he helps them to track down Morpheus. Thomas refuses to co-operate and demands the legal right of a phone call. 'Tell me, Mr Anderson,' quips Smith. 'What good is a phone call if you're unable to speak?' Thomas's mouth appears to literally seal itself shut, and he begins to panic. The other Agents in the room hold Thomas down as Smith gets out a small electronic device. This device changes before Thomas's eyes into a kind of robotic crustacean, before proceeding to bury itself directly into Thomas's stomach via his navel.

Thomas wakes with a start from a bad dream. Did he imagine everything? Just then his phone rings – it's Morpheus. He tells Thomas that he is The One: 'You may have spent the last few years looking for me, but I have spent my entire life looking for you.' Morpheus tells Thomas to go to the Adams Street Bridge. There he is met by a car, containing Trinity and two other people. The other woman in the car demands at gunpoint that Thomas take off his shirt. Trinity activates a bizarre-looking device above Thomas's navel, which extracts the metallic bug from his stomach. 'Jesus Christ! That thing's real?!' shrieks Thomas. Trinity dumps the bug out of the car window and they head off to meet Morpheus.

Morpheus greets Thomas as Neo, telling him that it's an honour to meet him. 'I imagine that right now you're feeling a bit like Alice, tumbling down the rabbit hole,' says Morpheus. He goes on to explain to Thomas why he's come to this meeting. 'You've felt it your entire life… that there's something wrong with the world. You don't know what it is – but it's there, like a splinter in your mind, driving you mad.' Thomas agrees with Morpheus – that's exactly what he feels. 'The Matrix?' asks Thomas. 'Do you want to know what it is?' enquires Morpheus. 'It is the world that has been pulled over your eyes to blind you from the truth.'

Morpheus goes on to explain that Neo, like everyone else, is a slave born into bondage, 'born into a prison that you cannot smell or taste or touch'. Morpheus then gives Thomas a choice. He presents him with two pills – a blue and a red pill.

If he takes the blue pill, he will continue to live his life as he has always done. If he takes the red pill, Morpheus will show Thomas 'how deep the rabbit hole goes'. Thomas reaches forward and takes the red pill. He follows Morpheus through into an adjacent room where a bank of electrical equipment has been set up. Trinity, the two people from the car and another man with a goatee are there also. As Trinity wires up Thomas to what appears to be a heart-rate monitor, Morpheus explains that the pill he took was a computer program, to pinpoint his location. When Thomas asks what this means, the man with the goatee quips, 'Buckle your seatbelt Dorothy 'cause Kansas is goin' bye-bye!'

> Thomas glances at a reflection of himself in a broken mirror. Suddenly the mirror appears to reform. Thomas touches it, and the reflective surface seems to absorb his finger, his arm, then his entire body…

He wakes up, inside a pink vat of goo. Evil-looking black tentacles are welded into parts of his body. He's hairless, naked, completely disoriented. He pulls a breathing tentacle out from his windpipe and takes in a huge gulp of air. He looks around and sees other humans, resting inside similar pink cocoons, asleep, unaware of where they are or what is happening to them. The cocoons are arranged in circular towers, hundreds of rows high, with sparks of electricity pulsing out from them. A gigantic robotic creature flies down from somewhere above him and observes that he has woken up. It grabs him by the throat and removes the connection plugged into the back of his skull. With that, all of the other black tendrils automatically disconnect themselves and a trap door opens in the base of his vat, flushing him downwards through a pipe and into a lake. Unable to swim, he begins to drown – until a much more primitive-looking claw descends from above and rescues him. Fading in and out of consciousness, he focuses on the face of Morpheus, who says in an almost tender, pitying way, 'Welcome to the real world.'

Slowly, the truth becomes apparent to Neo. His whole life up until this moment was not real. He's using his eyes for the first time in his life. Morpheus explains to Neo that the year isn't actually 1999 – it's close to 2199. They are on board Morpheus's ship, a hovercraft called the *Nebuchadnezzar*. Morpheus introduces the rest of his crew to Neo – Trinity, Apoc and Switch (who were in the car earlier), Cypher (with the goatee), and three new faces – brothers Tank and Dozer and a young boy aptly named Mouse.

Morpheus shows Neo what the Matrix is. Neo sits down in a chair on the flight deck of the *Nebuchadnezzar* and is then literally 'plugged in' via the connection welded into the back of his skull. He reappears inside a Construct – a virtual reality built as a loading program, where Morpheus and his crew are able to upload any information directly into their brains. Morpheus goes on to explain to Neo that the world he knew, the world at the end of the twentieth century, only exists 'as part of a neural-active simulation that we call the Matrix'. He then shows Neo what the world really looks like at the end of the twenty-second century – a blasted, derelict landscape of scorched earth and ruined buildings. 'Welcome to the desert of the real,' Morpheus says. Morpheus goes on to explain that in the early twenty-first century, mankind created AI – Artificial Intelligence. When mankind and machine declared war on each other, man tried to stop the monsters he had created by blocking out the sunlight, in the vain hope that cutting off their supply of solar energy would stop them. Instead the machines learned to adapt, and discovered that they could use a combination of fusion and the bio-electricity harnessed from the human body to survive. A horrified Neo is told that humans are now grown in vast fields, fed on the liquefied remains of the dead to keep them alive. 'The Matrix is a computer-generated dream world, built to keep us under control.'

Later, Morpheus tells Neo why he has received special treatment. 'When the Matrix was first built, there was a man born inside who had the ability to change whatever he wanted, to remake the Matrix as he saw fit. It was he who freed the first of us, taught us the truth. After he died, the Oracle prophesied his return.' Morpheus explains that he believes Neo is the reincarnation of the person who first learned the truth – he believes that Neo is The One, the only being who has the power to free humanity from the Matrix and to end the war between man and machine.

Neo finds out from Tank about the last remaining human city, Zion, where both the people who have escaped the Matrix and the natural-born humans now live. It's buried deep underground near the Earth's core in order to tap into the heat and energy still present there, as well as to hide from the marauding machines. Tank also shows Neo how to upload information into his brain – ju jitsu, kempo, tae kwon do, and many other forms of armed and unarmed combat. Neo tries to show off his new-found kung fu skills by fighting Morpheus, but despite his undoubted speed and skill the older man is able to beat him, simply because Neo hasn't been able to shake off the mindset of how the laws of gravity and physics should affect him. Morpheus shows Neo what he means by loading the 'jump program', something he tries with all of the people he frees from the Matrix. In it, Morpheus leaps in a single bound from the top of one skyscraper to the top of another one an impossible distance away. Like everyone else, Neo fails to make the jump on the first attempt. He learns an important lesson though – if your mind dies inside the Matrix, your body will die outside it.

The morality of their fight against the Matrix gets clouded for Neo when he discovers that although he may well be meeting the minds of real people that he's trying to help when inside the Matrix world, the fact that these people are connected to the system means that they should be thought of as working against the rebels – and when a policeman or member of the public is killed inside the Matrix, he or she will die in the real world too.

The problem is that the Matrix can control the people within it, and makes them try to stop the rebels at every opportunity. One way in which it can do this is via the Agents – specifically created sentient programs whose job it is to track down and eliminate errors in the system. The Agents can instantaneously take over any human still connected to the Matrix – so as Morpheus puts it, 'if you are not one of us, you are one of them'. Morpheus confides in a concerned Neo that every unplugged human that's ever stood their ground and fought an Agent has been killed. Despite this, Morpheus is confident that when the time comes, when he's ready, Neo will be powerful enough to defeat them.

Their training session is interrupted when the *Nebuchadnezzar* picks up an approaching Sentinel, a search-and-destroy machine nicknamed a 'squiddy'. Morpheus orders the ship to power down in order to hide from the Sentinel – luckily for them they are not discovered.

However, unbeknown to the rest of the crew, they are in mortal danger. Cypher shares a meal of juicy steak with Agent Smith in what appears to be an extremely posh restaurant. It was Cypher who was the Matrix's informant

> – and now he intends to complete his deal with it. 'After nine years, do you know what I realise? Ignorance is bliss.' Cypher's deal is this: he will be plugged back into the Matrix and become a famous and wealthy actor, with no memories of the 'real' world. In return, he will arrange for Morpheus to be handed over the Agents – with the knowledge he has (including the access codes to the mainframe computer protecting Zion), the machines will be able to win the war in no time at all.

Realising that Neo's training is at a suitable level, Morpheus decides that the time is right to take him to see the Oracle. With the exception of Tank and Dozer, who remain on board the *Nebuchadnezzar*, the rest of the crew plug themselves in and venture back into the Matrix... Trinity, Morpheus, Neo and Cypher set off to find the Oracle, leaving Mouse, Switch and Apoc to guard their exit point. However, Cypher surreptitiously leaves a switched-on mobile phone nearby... a signal for the Agents.

> In a run-down apartment block in the city, Neo finally gets to meet the Oracle, an elderly lady with a wicked sense of offbeat humour. He's rather taken aback when the Oracle asks him if he thinks that he is The One. Neo replies that he doesn't know. She tells him that being The One is like being in love – you just know if it's true. She looks at Neo and then

confirms what he already knows – although he has the gift, he isn't The One. She adds that he looks like he's waiting for something – his 'next life, maybe. Who knows?' She also warns him that he will have to make a choice – either Neo or Morpheus will die, and it will be Neo's decision.

Just as the car arrives back at the building containing the exit point, Neo experiences a flash of déjà vu. The others are deeply concerned – that's usually a signal that something in the Matrix has just been changed. As they run towards their exit point, they hear automatic gunfire from upstairs and Tank watches as Mouse's life signals cut out… he's dead. Dozens of armed police have surrounded the building and begin to close in on the rebels. Tank locates an alternative exit for them and points them in the right direction for their escape, down through the gap in between the walls. The rebels are part-way to freedom when Cypher sneezes, alerting a policeman to their presence. The cop is swiftly taken over by Agent Smith, who smashes through the wall and starts to choke Neo. Morpheus is appalled and throws himself through the wall and on top of Smith, shouting at Trinity to get Neo out. The others make their escape, but following a blistering fistfight with Agent Smith, Morpheus is captured.

Cypher, who had become separated from the rest of the escapees, manages to reach an exit point and return from inside the Matrix. Just as the others are about to reach the exit point, Cypher grabs a gun and shoots both Tank and Dozer. Trinity uses her mobile to contact the *Nebuchadnezzar* – and it's Cypher who picks up. He takes great pleasure in telling Trinity that he's betrayed them all and that he's chosen to go back into the Matrix, saying that he thinks the Matrix is more real than the 'real' world. Cypher pulls out the connections from the back of Apoc's and Switch's brains, severing the link between the real world and the Matrix and killing them both instantly. As he moves towards Neo – aiming to prove that the prophecy and everything about Morpheus's crusade is a lie – a badly wounded but still very much alive Tank blows him away. The exit-point phone rings, and both Trinity and Neo return to the *Nebuchadnezzar*.

Handcuffed to a chair in a room near the top of a city-centre skyscraper, Morpheus listens to Smith explain about the history of the Matrix. The first version of the Matrix was designed to keep humanity pacified and unquestioning thanks to an artificial reality where there was peace and happiness. However the human brain refused to believe in such a nirvana: 'as a species, human beings define their reality through misery and suffering.' Because the brains of the humans plugged into the Matrix refused to accept perfect happiness, it was redesigned to reflect the Earth in 1999, complete with all of its faults and flaws.

Tank realises that the machines are trying to break into Morpheus's mind, in order to retrieve the information about the Zion mainframe. The only thing they can do, in order to save the thousands upon thousands of people living there, is to sever the connection and kill Morpheus before his secrets are revealed. But before Tank can pull the plug, Neo stops him. He realises that this is the moment that the Oracle predicted, and that he has to make a choice. Neo chooses to go back into the Matrix and rescue Morpheus, because if he isn't really The One, then it won't matter if he dies – whereas it will matter if Morpheus is killed. When Neo confesses to Trinity that the Oracle told him that he wasn't The One, Trinity is baffled and tells him that it can't be true, but refuses to explain why. Neo goes to plug himself back in, followed by a very determined Trinity.

Left alone with Morpheus, Smith makes an astonishing confession. He hates being inside the Matrix. He can't stand it any longer, comparing it to a zoo populated by an out-of-control virus. He tells Morpheus that he can taste humanity's stink, and that he's beginning to fear that he's being infected by it. 'I must get free,' he hisses. Smith hopes that the key to his freedom is hidden inside Morpheus's mind – once Zion has been destroyed, there will be no reason for him to have to stay in the Matrix any longer.

Downstairs, Neo and Trinity shoot their way through dozens of heavily armed security guards as they make their way towards the lifts to rescue Morpheus. Inside the lift, Trinity arms an enormous explosive device. They cut the wires to the lift and use the reverse momentum of a lift cable to propel themselves up to the top floor. On the roof of the building they are confronted by an Agent, who releases a clipful of bullets at Neo. Neo moves so fast that he is able to dodge the bullets, astonishing Trinity (who managed to kill the Agent while it was distracted). Tank uploads a pilot's program into Trinity's brain so that she can pilot the helicopter that's sitting on the rooftop. Hovering adjacent to the room where the Agents are holding Morpheus, Neo uses the on-board machine gun to blow away the agents. Morpheus breaks free of his chains and dives through the now open window towards the helicopter. Realising that Morpheus can't jump all the way from the building to the 'copter, Neo launches himself out of the helicopter and grabs Morpheus. The pair of them plummet to the ground, only saved by the rope attaching Neo to the helicopter. As Trinity pilots the 'copter away, an Agent shoots the fuel tank and the helicopter begins to spin out of control. Morpheus and Neo jump to safety on to the roof of a nearby building, and Trinity manages to save herself by letting go of the controls, severing the rope attached to Neo, and grabbing on to it herself. The helicopter explodes into the side of a nearby tower block, and Neo pulls Trinity to safety. As the trio heads towards the nearest exit point, Smith is delighted to discover that they've been able to trace the location of the *Nebuchadnezzar*, and orders an attack by Sentinels.

In a subway station, the trio locate their exit point and Morpheus returns to his ship. Just as Trinity returns, Smith shoots the telephone receiver and traps Neo. Smith and Neo launch into a ferocious fistfight. 'I'm going to enjoy watching you die, Mr Anderson,' sneers the Agent. Neo finally appears to be beginning to believe the extent of his abilities, but the fight doesn't go all his way. Dazed by Smith's punches, Neo is flung into the path of an oncoming train. He manages to jump out of the way just in time and makes his escape.

On board the *Nebuchadnezzar*, the Sentinels are closing in on them – there are maybe five minutes until they arrive. Tank tries to direct

Neo to the nearest exit – unfortunately it's through a street full of people, many of whom morph into Agents. Neo races from building to building, pursued all the time by still more Agents. At the same time, the Sentinels arrive at the *Nebuchadnezzar* and begin to cut their way into the ship.

Neo arrives at his exit point – it's in the Heart o' the City Hotel, where Trinity was nearly caught by the Agents. Tank directs him to room 303, where the exit-point phone is. By now, the Sentinels have broken through the hull and are inside the ship. Although the *Nebuchadnezzar* has an electromagnetic pulse weapon, they can't use it until Neo has returned safely from the Matrix, or they will kill him.

Neo bursts through the door of room 303 – only to find himself facing Smith and a fully loaded gun. Smith shoots him through the chest at point-blank range, before emptying his entire gun into Neo. On board the ship, Neo's life-signs flatline. A grief-stricken Trinity leans in to kiss Neo's body. She whispers to him that he can't be dead, because the Oracle predicted that she would fall in love with The One. She says he can't be dead, 'because I love you. You hear me? I love you'. Trinity places a delicate kiss on Neo's lips...

…and suddenly his life-signs spring to life. 'Now get up,' she commands. Inside the Matrix, Smith is astonished when Neo gets up from the floor. As Smith and two other Agents open fire on him, Neo raises his right hand. The bullets from their guns simply stop in mid air before falling to the floor. Tank, watching these events unfold on his monitor screens, simply asks, 'How?' 'He is The One,' replies Morpheus. Neo can now see the Matrix's code for what it is – strings of green data in the shape of walls, people, Agents. Smith runs to fight him, but Neo is in another class altogether. Neo jumps inside Smith, and rips the program apart. Neo gets to the exit point and his consciousness returns to his body on board the *Nebuchadnezzar* just as Morpheus triggers his EMP to wipe out the Sentinels.

Some time later, back inside the Matrix, Neo makes a phone call to the machines, the Matrix, the system. He promises that he is going to show humanity a world without the rules and structures of the Matrix. Neo hangs up the phone and walks into the middle of a crowd of people. Suddenly, miraculously, The One zooms vertically upwards, soaring towards the sky like a rocket.

| The Matrix: Reloaded |

Neo dreams – a horrifying, terrible dream in which Trinity, desperately trying to escape from a trap within the Matrix, is cornered by Agents. After a fierce gunfight, Trinity falls from a great height, pumping bullets back at her pursuer. As she falls, a single bullet pierces her chest and she winces in agony…

Now awake and on board the *Nebuchadnezzar*, Neo is comforted by Trinity, who asks him if he wants to talk about his nightmares. Neo says that he just wishes he knew what to do – she tells him that 'she' will call, and that he's not to worry.

A meeting takes place inside the Matrix between several of the captains and crews of ships working for the free people of Zion. A beautiful female captain called Niobe confirms the worst news to her comrades: the machines have found the location of Zion, and that they are burrowing downwards, intent on wiping out Zion completely. At current estimates, in 72 hours time, 250,000 Sentinels will be in place to launch an all-out attack: one Sentinel for every man, woman and child alive on Zion. Commander Lock, the man in charge of co-ordinating Zion's defence, has ordered all ships back to base in order to mount a last-ditch attempt to protect the city from the machines.

However Morpheus is deeply concerned by this last order – if they return to Zion, they will be out of broadcast range of the Matrix, and may therefore miss any communications that the Oracle might have for The One. Morpheus knows that the *Nebuchadnezzar* urgently needs to be recharged, so he's happy to return back to Zion immediately. But he asks one of the other captains to disobey Lock's order and remain outside Zion in order to pick up any transmissions from the Oracle. Somewhat begrudgingly, Captain Ballard agrees to stay behind – if only to see what Lock (or as Ballard calls him, 'Deadlock') will do to Morpheus for this act of open insubordination.

The meeting is interrupted by the arrival of Agent Smith. Surprisingly, Smith makes no attempt to wipe out the meeting – instead he leaves a present for Neo, as a 'gift' for setting him free. However, Smith is closely followed by yet more Agents, who do attempt to wipe out the humans attending the meeting. Thanks to Neo's presence, everyone is able to escape and Neo is able to show off his massively increased skills. Observing the battle, Agent Smith talks to... another Agent Smith. They agree with each other that everything seems to be going as expected.

Arriving back at Zion, the *Nebuchadnezzar* docks and begins recharging. As the crew is being marched to see Commander Lock, Neo asks Trinity what the deal is between Lock and Morpheus. Trinity explains that the problem is Niobe – she used to go out with

Morpheus, now she goes out with Lock. It seems that their relationship fell apart after Morpheus visited the Oracle. Neo wryly comments that visiting the Oracle tends to change things.

Trinity and Neo are approached by a young and very enthusiastic kid. The kid offers to carry Neo's bags for him, saying that Neo was responsible for freeing him from the Matrix. The kid tells them that as soon as he's old enough, he plans to join the crew of the *Nebuchadnezzar*. It's clear that the kid has a severe case of hero-worship towards Trinity, and especially towards Neo.

Morpheus is hauled over the coals by Lock. He demands that Morpheus explain his actions – Morpheus simply replies by saying that there is only one way to save Zion, and that's by ensuring The One has all the information he needs. Lock is furious and shouts at Morpheus that not everybody believes in the prophecy of The One. Just then, Councillor Hamann arrives to speak to Lock. He advises Lock that the rumours circulating throughout Zion about 'something big' being about to happen must be addressed. Lock suggests that at tonight's Temple Gathering they do not reveal the full extent of the imminent threat, and they will therefore avoid a panic amongst the population. Hamann asks Morpheus for his view – Morpheus suggests that the best thing to do is be honest. There is nothing to fear, because the machines will never reach the gates of Zion – The One will prevent that.

Realising that it will take 24 to 36 hours to fully recharge the *Nebuchadnezzar*, Trinity and Neo head back to their quarters hoping for some romantic time together. However as they approach their room they are greeted by crowds of hopeful pilgrims, all keen for Neo to give his blessing to either themselves or their loved ones. Neo still seems to be finding his role as the Messiah a difficult one.

Link, the new Operator on board the *Nebuchadnezzar*, has returned home to his wife Zee. They have visitors – Cas (Dozer's widow and Zee's sister-in-law) and her two children. Once they leave, Zee rounds on Link, criticising his faith in Morpheus. She tells Link that she's already lost two brothers on the *Nebuchadnezzar* and has no intention of losing her husband. She urges Link to be careful, and he promises that he will – especially now that he's seen with his own eyes some of the things of which Neo is capable.

Later that night, inside a huge underground cavern, Morpheus addresses the Temple Gathering. The thousands of people present hang on his every word. He tells the crowd not to be afraid. Yes, the machines have raised an army, but for the past hundred years they have tried to wipe out humanity and they have failed. The crowd laps up Morpheus's words, and spins into an almost trance-like frenzy of dancing, singing and chanting.

Neo wakes from yet another nightmare – it's always the same one, of Trinity taking a bullet in the chest and falling to her death. Unable to sleep any more, Neo goes for a walk. He bumps into Councillor Hamann, and together they wander down to the engineering level of Zion. They ponder the nature of control and the irony that Zion still needs machines to provide the air and the water for humanity to survive – and yet, they face extinction from another group of machines.

The next morning, a message arrives from Captain Ballard – the Oracle has been in touch and needs to speak to Neo. As the crew prepares to depart, a man called Bane – who has somehow been physically infected by the now rogue Agent Smith – moves as if to attack Neo. However, the presence of other people dissuades him and he simply says, 'I just wanted to catch you to say good luck'. At the same time, the kid gives Neo a present from 'one of the orphans' as a good luck charm. Much to Lock's dismay, Councillor Hamann has given the

Nebuchadnezzar clearance to leave. When Lock protests that he needs every ship to defend Zion, Hamann tells him that Zion's survival 'depends on more than how many ships we have'.

Venturing inside the Matrix again, Neo encounters a white-clad man called Seraph. Seraph offers to take Neo to see the Oracle, but first insists on fighting him, to ensure that Neo really is The One. After a brief fight, Seraph concurs that Neo is who he says he is, and takes Neo through a 'back door' into an outdoor courtyard where the Oracle is waiting to speak to him.

Neo asks the Oracle if she is in fact a program rather than a real person. She confirms that both she and her protector Seraph are in fact sentient programs. This makes Neo question how he can trust her – if she's a program, how can he be sure that she isn't working for the Matrix? 'The bad news is there's no way if you can really know whether I'm here to help you or not,' she says. 'So it's really up to you. You just have to make up your own damn mind to either accept what I'm going to tell you, or reject it.' The Oracle goes on to explain in more detail how the Matrix works. Every element of the Matrix, such as birds flying, has a program which controls its function. Programs that work effectively are never really seen or noticed. It's only when programs start to misbehave that they become obvious. All legends of ghosts, werewolves, vampires and so on are cases of the Matrix trying to rewrite rogue programs. The Oracle goes on to explain what happens to these rogue programs. 'Usually a program chooses exile when it faces deletion,' she says – or sometimes they return to the Source, the machine mainframe, the very heart of the Matrix itself. The Oracle tells Neo that he must go to the Source, the doorway of light that he sees in his dreams.

> Neo asks her about his dreams, specifically the one about Trinity's death. He's puzzled – if he has the sight, why can't he see what happens to Trinity when she falls? Can he choose whether she lives or dies? The Oracle tells him that he's already made that choice: 'Now you have to understand it.' What if he fails? he asks. 'Then Zion will fall.' She explains that in order to access the Source, Neo will need to find the Keymaker. Missing for many years, the Keymaker's location has just been identified. He's being held captive by a very old and very dangerous program called the Merovingian. Seraph interrupts Neo and the Oracle's conversation, ushering her away to safety. Just after she leaves, Neo is greeted by his old nemesis, Agent Smith.

Smith is joined by copy after copy after copy of himself. The Smiths explain to Neo that although he destroyed the original Smith, something unusual happened. Smith decided not to go back to the System, but to remain as a free program. Somehow Smith and Neo are connected. Smith confronts Neo and tries to take from Neo the one thing that he no longer has – a sense of purpose. That purpose now is to kill Neo. Smith after Smith joins in the fist-fight against Neo. For a short while it seems that Neo is being overwhelmed by the army of Smiths, but eventually Neo shakes them off in one swift movement and rockets to safety.

Back in Zion, concern grows for the fate of The One and the *Nebuchadnezzar*. Having heard nothing from them, the Council decides to send two ships to search for the lost crew – much to the fury of Lock. Captain Soren of the *Vigilant* and then Captain Niobe of the Logos agree to take part in the search.

Inside the Matrix, in a restaurant called 'Le Vrai', Neo, Trinity and Morpheus face the Merovingian. He speaks in a French accent and has a very superior attitude towards the humans. The Merovingian introduces the rebels to his wife, a stunningly beautiful woman called Persephone. Sitting with them at the dining table are twins with dreadlocked white hair. Neo tells the Merovingian that he's come for the Keymaker. The Merovingian snorts with derision – he tells Neo that he's simply following the Oracle's orders; he hasn't made a choice of his own in coming here. He tells Neo that he has no intention whatsoever of giving up the Keymaker.

When the Merovingian leaves the table to go 'for a piss', Persephone tells Neo to follow her if he wants to find the Keymaker. Going through the restaurant's kitchens and into a secret room, Persephone promises to give them the Keymaker if Neo will kiss her, passionately, like he does with Trinity. Despite Trinity's misgivings, Neo complies. 'Aaah yes,' she sighs, 'that's it. I envy you. But such a thing is not meant to last.' Persephone kills one of the two guards protecting the Keymaker and sends the other one back to tell her husband what she's done.

As Trinity and Morpheus try to get the Keymaker to safety, the Merovingian's goons arrive and a massive battle breaks out. Neo eventually wipes out most of them, but as he tries to flee with the others, a magical door transports him to a temple high on the top of a mountain, some 500 miles north of the others. Neo flies back towards the city, Link guiding him as best he can.

Meanwhile, Trinity and Morpheus are doing their best to get the Keymaker out of the Matrix and to freedom. Pursued by the Merovingian's gun-toting twins, they decide on a very risky manoeuvre – an escape along one of the city's freeways. After a bone-crunching battle with policemen, Agents and the twins, Trinity, Morpheus and the Keymaker are rescued thanks to the timely intervention of Neo and Niobe, whose ship and crew have arrived to assist The One.

The Keymaker tells the rebels about one special building within the Matrix. It's covered by high-security systems, but through one door, on one special floor, it's possible to access the System itself. The rebels formulate a plan – blow up the electricity supplies to the city, and in the 314 seconds before the security systems are reactivated, The One must go through the door into the System.

Realising that this plan may have something to do with the dreams he's been having of Trinity's death, Neo makes her promise that no matter what happens, she won't go into the Matrix. Trinity agrees.

The plan seems to go smoothly until the team sent to blow up the city's power supply is wiped out. Realising that the security systems on the building will still be active and therefore lethal to Neo and the Keymaker, Trinity has no option but to go into the Matrix herself and carry out the sabotage on the power station. She manages this with just seconds to spare. However the act of sabotage draws the attention of a number of Agents, who begin to pursue her.

Approaching the secret entrance to the Source, Morpheus, the Keymaker and Neo are shocked to be confronted by dozens of Agent Smiths. Neo and Morpheus manage to fight their way into the access room to the Source, but the Keymaker is mortally wounded. As Morpheus uses one door to return to the real world, Neo uses the Keymaker's key to access the Source.

Inside the Source, Neo meets an elderly looking man. 'I am the Architect,' he says. 'I created the Matrix. I've been waiting for you.'

To Neo's horror, the Architect seems quite happy to see him. The Architect explains that this isn't the first time that 'The One' has fought his way through to the Source, intent on destroying the Matrix. In fact, it's the sixth time. He tells a disbelieving Neo that because of the flaws inherent in the construction of the Matrix, every time the system is rebooted, the program will automatically run until the prophecy is released and an individual believing himself to be The One arrives at the Source. It's fate, totally and utterly.

The Architect goes on to reveal to Neo that the population of Zion is about to be wiped out. That's the way it always happens. It will be the sixth time that Zion and its entire population has been destroyed. The Architect reveals to Neo what his purpose *really* is. As The One, he *is* the saviour of mankind. It's his job to select the sixteen females and seven males that will be required to rebuild Zion for the seventh time. If he doesn't comply with these demands and essentially reboot the system, then there will be a cataclysmic system crash – not only will everyone in Zion be exterminated, but every human plugged into the Matrix will die also, bringing about the extinction of the human race.

The Architect watches Neo's reactions to this shocking news, and observes that his responses are different to those he's observed on the previous five 'Ones' – notably because on this occasion, Neo's love for Trinity seems to be changing the rules. The Architect shows Neo what *is* happening to Trinity – she's cornered on the top floor of a building... the same building that Neo knows she will plummet to her death from. The Architect taunts Neo still further. He shows Neo two doors. One will lead him into the Source, where the system will reboot, the humans in Zion will die, but humanity will be saved. The other door will lead him back into the Matrix, where Trinity will die and where, as a result of the failure to reboot, all human life will be terminated. Neo chooses to go back into the Matrix.

Link and Morpheus watch as Neo flies, faster than anything ever recorded, to try to save Trinity's life. Although he catches her before she hits the ground, he's too late to stop the bullet entering her chest. Neo cradles Trinity in his arms as she dies. Refusing to accept her death, Neo reaches inside Trinity, and miraculously pulls out the bullet from her corpse. She wakes, and they embrace.

Back on board the *Nebuchadnezzar*, Morpheus is finding it hard to comprehend that the prophecy was a lie. The One has entered the Source, but the war is not over. Neo tells Morpheus that unless they do something, Zion will be destroyed within 24 hours. Link notices a gang of Sentinels heading towards them, and attempts to pilot the ship to safety. At that point, a bomb rips through the *Nebuchadnezzar* and it plummets on to the barren surface of the Earth, smashed beyond repair.

The rebels survive the crash and scramble from the wreckage, trying to take cover from the approaching Sentinels. However, Neo stops, turns round and – seemingly using the powers of The One that only work inside the Matrix – stops the Sentinels in their tracks. The effort of this knocks Neo into a coma.

Some time later, and a group of survivors are discussing what happened. The machines did burrow their way into Zion. Most of humanity is now dead. A few survivors managed to get on to ships and are now trying to regroup. The only survivor of the slaughter of Zion was Bane – the man now linked to Agent Smith...

What do you dO?

Within the universe of *The Matrix*, we've been introduced to a wide variety of extremely different characters. How they've grown and changed throughout the two films (so far) is a pivotal element as to why the films are so entertaining. Here we look at the principal three characters, their motivations, and highlight some of their finest moments.

Neo/Thomas Anderson: At the start of *The Matrix*, we're introduced to a sad, lonely computer hacker called Thomas Anderson, a man seemingly completely adrift in his life. Thomas spends his day in a dead-end job for a major international software company, and although we're told he works in some kind of programming role, the precise nature of what Thomas does remains a mystery. What does he actually program? What does the company do? These details are never filled in, but that lack of clarity actually adds to the feeling of disassociation that Thomas seems to be suffering from. When he's given a severe telling off by his boss for being late for work, it really does appear that Thomas couldn't give a damn. This disconnection from the 'real' world helps to emphasise and reinforce Thomas's growing realisation that something isn't right with the world, a feeling that shortly comes to a head when he encounters the mysterious Trinity and Morpheus.

We do learn more about Thomas's other secret life though. When Thomas is at home late one night, he's visited by a group of fellow computer hackers. Thomas seems to be acting as some kind of information dealer, passing vital bits of technology to people who can afford to pay for it. The analogy with drug dealing is quite clearly drawn – he makes appointments for people to call by, the 'stuff' is hidden carefully within his apartment, and he warns his customers not to get caught with it. Hardly the behaviour of a messiah for humanity, really.

Above all though, it's Thomas's natural curiosity that leads him into discovering his real life, his true identity. The teasing clues left for him by Trinity and Morpheus pique that curiosity, leading him to 'follow the white rabbit' and eventually to choose to take the red pill. Again, we're touching upon the theme of drug abuse here – remember that as far as Thomas Anderson is concerned, he has absolutely no idea what is contained inside the drug that he's just swallowed. Popping pills that have been given to you by a complete stranger can hardly be classed as a sensible activity.

When Neo wakes up in the real world, his first response is one of shock and denial. To have every memory and experience that you've lived during your whole life wrenched away must be a traumatic experience, and indeed we later discover that freeing adults from *The Matrix* is something that is very rarely attempted simply because their brains are unable to readjust to their new reality. Simply accepting that he's no longer on the earth of 1999 is hard enough, but when Morpheus shows Neo a representation of the scorched and shattered surface of the planet and the truth about mankind's slavery, he finds it very difficult to take. This is a character trait that Neo reveals time and time again – a reluctance to accept the truth of his situation and what is happening to his friends. The most obvious example of this comes when Neo discovers his destiny to become The One.

Being told that you are the sole person who can liberate the whole of humanity from slavery has got to be an incredible pressure, and on this occasion it's hardly surprising that

Neo finds it difficult to believe. Neo knows that he has some special ability within *The Matrix*, skills that the others find difficult to match. But when the Oracle tells him that he isn't The One, Neo is relieved: the burden of responsibility (for someone who had always been a slacker in his former life) has been lifted from his shoulders. Despite this relief, Neo still feels as though he has an important part to play in the struggle against the Matrix, and he carries on fighting alongside the rest of the rebels in their struggle. Eventually events conspire to force Neo into making a decision that will effect the rest of his life. Told by the Oracle that either he or Morpheus will die, Neo makes a critical choice. Knowing that he can't possibly be The One, Neo decides to do something useful with his life and willingly returns to the Matrix in an attempt to rescue Morpheus from the clutches of the machines, believing that Morpheus must carry on living because of his destiny to be the one to locate The One.

This self-sacrifice is of course a vital development for Neo. Following the metaphor of Neo as the messiah, the saviour of humanity, Neo has to die and be resurrected. Just as Jesus Christ allowed himself to be sacrificed, so Neo realises that if he goes back into the Matrix, the chances are that he won't come out alive. When Agent Smith's bullets rip into him, the one thing that Neo is happy to take to his grave is the knowledge that at the very least he's done something to help fight the good fight.

Of course, Neo's story only begins there. Following his resurrection as The One, Neo seems almost blissful, as though he's seeing the world in its truth and reality for the very first time. He playfully bats away the bullets of the Agents, toys with Smith before literally ripping him apart, and then does a canny impression of Superman just for the sake of it. He even places a telephone call to the Matrix, threatening that he will soon be able to bring about its downfall. Flash forward six months later to the events at the start of *The Matrix: Reloaded*, and it's a completely different Neo that we see. This Neo is still doubtful, he's still unsure of his new strength and abilities. What could have brought about this sudden shift from ultra-confident to cautious? Well, although we never see it happen, the death of Tank might well have had something to do with this personality shift. At the end of *The Matrix*, Tank is still very much alive and kicking (although wounded thanks to Cypher's treachery), but he's long dead in *The Matrix: Reloaded*. Perhaps Neo blames himself for Tank's death? Certainly Tank's sister Zee blames Morpheus and his crew for Tank's demise. Could it be that a bout of overconfidence in his new abilities led to a tragic death? It certainly would explain why Neo has stopped having absolute faith in his abilities and why the dreams of Trinity's death have begun to disturb him so much.

Neo's romance with Trinity seems to spring directly from the Oracle's prophecy – because she foretold that Trinity would fall in love with The One it appears to just happen. We don't get to see the evolution of their romance

> in between the first two movies, but it all seems a little bit fast-paced. Of course, the threat of imminent death is a marvellous aphrodisiac, so perhaps that's being a little judgemental. This love for Trinity helps Neo to face his fears and therefore to carry on doing his job – finding a way of accessing the Source and defeating the Matrix. However, during the final assault on the headquarters of the Source, Neo begs Trinity not to re-enter the Matrix, fearful for her safety because of his dreams.

When the Architect confronts Neo with the terrible truth about the nature of the Matrix and The One – that the entire prophecy is a lie and that Zion is always destined to be wiped out and reborn, Neo once again finds it very hard to believe. Yet again he makes a crucial decision that will have a huge impact on the future of the whole of humanity – when faced with the choice of following the traditional path of The One and opting to save humanity via rebooting the Matrix or allowing a catastrophic systems failure and possibly the destruction of the entire human race simply to save Trinity's life, Neo opts for the latter. It's his love for Trinity that forces him into making that decision, one that intrigues the seemingly unflappable Architect. Neo races to save Trinity's life, but tragically he's too late – a bullet has ripped into her chest and she dies in his arms. Just as Trinity's love for Neo brings him back from the grave, so Neo's love for Trinity plays its part in resurrecting her too. Both events appear to have no precedent within the Matrix, particularly since Trinity is just an ordinary mortal, with no super powers of her own. Neo looks surprised by his new ability, to bring back from the dead those killed inside the Matrix. Surely this will prove to be an extremely valuable ability in his later battle with the machines.

Shocked, elated and devastated in equal measures, Neo reels from the realisation that he's managed to save his love, but has that come at the cost of the lives of all humans both inside and outside the Matrix? When the *Nebuchadnezzar* is downed, Neo is shaken once more, especially as a Sentinel approaches intent on killing the survivors. For a moment, Neo appears confused – he tells his colleagues that something feels different to him. He stops fleeing from the machine, turns around and uses what seem to be the powers of The One (which up until that point had only ever been active when inside the computer-generated world of the Matrix) to stop the lethal machine in its hovering tracks. By the end of *The Matrix: Reloaded*, we have yet to discover what effect this sudden arrival of new skills and abilities will have on Neo, as he lies unconscious in a coma. Will he now gain the confidence required to defeat the machines forever? Judging by the few clips of *The Matrix: Revolutions* seen in the trailer, this could very well be the case...

Trinity: The prevailing image of Trinity from *The Matrix* films is of an ice-cool, PVC-clad gun-toting momma with a bad attitude. Indeed, when we first see her, she manages to polish off a room full of policemen in the blink of an eye. However, underneath this cool and calm exterior, Trinity is a desperate woman. Part of a rag-tag group of rebels constantly on the run from an army of lethal machines, Trinity will do whatever she has to do to survive, but it appears that she's definitely running low on the faith and commitment that she's always been able to rely upon.

During the initial meetings she has with Thomas Anderson, Trinity maintains an air of supreme confidence and that same determination to convince Thomas that taking the red pill is the right thing to do. Trinity is driven largely by the urgings of her leader and captain, Morpheus. We don't get to see a great deal of the workings of Trinity's own mind as she believes totally in her leader's goals. When Neo is rescued from the Matrix, Trinity's initial reaction towards him is wary to say the least. When she's challenged by the ever-cynical Cypher, Trinity refuses to be drawn on whether or not Neo is The One. Indeed, it's only when she sees what Neo is capable of with her own eyes that she throws her own allegiance completely behind him.

Slowly, Trinity begins to fall in love with Neo – or perhaps in the first instance, in love with what Neo represents: freedom, liberty, the fulfilment of what has been prophesied. Fiercely loyal to Morpheus, when Neo agrees to re-enter the Matrix to save his life, Trinity doesn't hesitate for a moment and joins him, even threatening to pull rank on him if he tries to stop her. This is the behaviour of a true warrior, someone willing to fight and die for the cause she believes in. It's no wonder that Neo finds emotional and military support in her presence. When Neo is killed by Agent Smith's bullets, it is Trinity's kiss that revives him. She begs for him not to be dead and finally vocalises what the Oracle had foretold for her – that she would fall in love with The One. This immense mutual love and respect will come back to Trinity in a very real way at the end of *The Matrix: Reloaded* when she faces a similar fate herself.

But moving back for a moment to the relationship she and Neo enjoy at the beginning of *Reloaded*, it's intriguing to see where the real power in their relationship lies. With Neo deflated and de-motivated, it's up to Trinity to reassure and empower her boyfriend. Rather than behaving in the role of a warrior, Trinity has now assumed the function of a traditional girlfriend, being there for the hero and (somewhat more worrying for a feminist reading of *The Matrix* films) ending up as a damsel in distress that needs to be saved by the love of a good man.

Thankfully though, Trinity doesn't devolve into a typical female character in an action movie. She uses all of her strength, skill and determination during the high-speed motorway chase, placing herself in mortal danger many times so that the Keymaker can get to safety. Later, when Neo asks her not to re-enter the Matrix, Trinity agrees, merely taking Neo's word. Although this shows a great deal of trust on Trinity's part (to go against all of her training so far, and her innate desire to take part in all of the attacks upon the Matrix) she's forced to make a snap decision when the initial group of rebels trying to take out the power supply is killed. It's Trinity's decision to re-enter the Matrix that directly causes Neo's decision when talking with the Source. If Trinity had obeyed Neo's instructions, it's almost certain that Neo would have chosen differently and may have decided to sacrifice the majority of the humans in Zion in order to ensure the survival of humanity. Trinity's involvement in that equation will undoubtedly have major ramifications in *The Matrix: Revolutions*.

Morpheus: As a determined leader, Morpheus is inspirational, passionate and resolute. His first appearances at the start of *The Matrix* give very little evidence of the man we discover through the rest of the films. Initially, Morpheus seems little more than a thinker, literally the brains behind the outfit. However all of this is shattered when we see Morpheus training Neo inside the simulation program – this is one seriously dangerous dude!

Morpheus tells Neo that he has been searching for The One his whole life. But is this really the case? Could he perhaps be 'bigging up' his own part? In *Reloaded*, we discover that Morpheus was in a relationship with Niobe, until he visited the Oracle and changed his life. Presumably this visit was when he was told that it was his destiny to locate The One. So unless Morpheus began dating at a particularly precocious age, I believe we have to take as read the fact that Morpheus isn't averse to twisting the truth when it's needed to achieve a more important goal. Just as he tells Neo that he's been searching for The One all his life, Morpheus later proudly tells the population of Zion not to worry because the machines will never breach their defences. Once again, he's making claims that he really has no way of backing up.

Despite these flaws, Morpheus does what every good general needs to do. He inspires his troops and leads from the front, never expecting his followers to do anything he wouldn't do himself. When the rebels are attempting to flee from the Agent trap set up by Cypher, Morpheus willingly throws himself on top of Agent Smith in an attempt to allow the others to escape. This results in a brutal interrogation at the hands of the Agents, during which a brain-scanning program is injected into the virtual Morpheus inside the Matrix. Thankfully for the population of Zion, Morpheus is able to fight off the effects of the program/drug until Neo and Trinity are able to mount a rescue attempt.

Morpheus is seen to be visibly elated by the progress that Neo makes as The One. When it seems for a short while that Neo has been killed, Morpheus cannot believe what he is seeing – this shatters and undermines everything he's believed and makes no sense to him at all. When Neo rises again, Morpheus's faith is repaid in full. Having seen the prophecy come true, Morpheus's belief in the prophecy and in the complete ability of The One to liberate humanity is stronger than ever. Perhaps this explains why at the start of *Reloaded*, Morpheus is almost tranquil. He behaves in a calm, rational, even laid-back fashion when challenged by the Councillors in Zion to defend his decisions. It never even begins to cross Morpheus's mind that he could be wrong – his faith that the prophecy will be fulfilled is absolute.

When Morpheus assists Neo in fighting his way into the Source of the Matrix, he honestly believes that the war will soon be over. The news that Neo brings back from the Architect is shattering for him. It seems as though the prophecy that he has based his whole life upon has been a lie, a deliberate fabrication created by the Architect and the Oracle to give rebellious elements something to believe in. To suddenly discover that what you believed to be free will was in fact all pre-ordained is a crushing blow to Morpheus. He's shattered, unable to

> believe in what Neo has told him. When the *Nebuchadnezzar* crashes to the surface of the earth, it's all that Morpheus can do simply to flee for his life. He's no longer the brave, fearless leader – he's just a man on the run. It will take a huge demonstration of power from Neo, or a rapid readjustment in mental attitude, for Morpheus to reclaim his position as a vital general in the fight against the machines. But with Zion and its occupants apparently now wiped out as well, what does Morpheus still have to fight for?

With the rules that he's been playing by now ripped up and torn apart, will Morpheus be able to refocus on the battle at hand – preventing the catastrophic systems failure predicted by the Architect, a failure that will wipe out all of the humans connected to the Matrix as well as the ones that have already died in Zion?

What's in a Name?

For any movie to be successfully 'cool', one of the first elements to get right is the choice of suitably enigmatic, sophisticated or just plain outrageous names for the main characters. Getting the names wrong could make even the most exciting action scenes laughable – for instance, imagine how ludicrous it would have sounded to have had Barry Higginson rescuing Princess Doris from the clutches of the evil Lord of the Sith, Darth Eric. However, a clever writer will always have a reason for selecting their names – and the Wachowski Brothers made their choices very carefully indeed. Not only are all of the character names in *The Matrix* cool and unusual, they also reveal a great deal about who the characters actually *are*, and how they may develop. How can a name reveal this? Well, it's just a question of investigating a little bit into classical myths and legends...

Just as most modern first names in Western culture had their origins in Latin or Greek, many of the characters in the *Matrix* films are named after gods, heroes, places and other elements from the legends of Greece and Rome. Other names also come from historical people and places. By examining the stories behind those legendary characters and events, we can discover more about *The Matrix* and perhaps even predict what's going to happen in the third film, *The Matrix: Revolutions*... Here's an A to Z guide to some of the names in *The Matrix* that have the most pertinent derivations...

Apoc: 'Apoc' is an abbreviation for the last book of the Bible, the Book of the Apocalypse. Of course, the apocalypse is the end of the world – the time when everything comes to a final conclusion. However, despite its nasty-sounding connotations, the word 'apocalypse' does not necessarily mean 'catastrophe': although this is its most common usage, its literal meaning (from the original Greek) is a prophecy or revelation – and the Book of the Apocalypse is now usually renamed the Book of Revelations. To many Christians, the Book of Revelations is a source of great comfort – knowing that the righteous and faithful will indeed reach paradise at the end of the world. An extra note of interest – in the Book of Revelations, the place where the faithful of Israel will gather before ascending into heaven is on Mount Zion...

Cypher: Conventionally spelt with an 'i' rather than a 'y', 'cipher' means 'zero', 'one that has no weight, worth, or influence: a nonentity', and also 'a method of transforming a text in order to conceal its meaning; to encode' . As Cypher's true allegiances were hidden for some time, this makes perfect sense. Cypher felt like he was nobody – although he knew the truth about the nature of the Matrix, Cypher wished that he could erase that knowledge, that he could become a nobody once again. To this end, Cypher betrayed his comrades simply because he couldn't imagine a life as pointless and hopeless as the reality he was faced with – in his view, the fictional world was preferable to the horrific reality he had to face every day.

Of course, any character in literature who betrays his comrades – and specifically one who betrays the hero or Christ figure – will usually find himself being compared to Judas Iscariot. In the New Testament of the Bible, we discover that one of Jesus Christ's leading followers (or Apostles) betrayed him to the Roman authorities for thirty pieces of silver. As a direct result, Jesus was captured and executed by the Romans. Three days later, Christ rose from the dead to continue his work. Once again, these biblical stories are reflected in *The Matrix*. When Trinity's kiss miraculously resurrects Neo, he comes back to life in Room 303... a room number that represents Cypher's 'thirty pieces of silver' and the three days before the resurrection. A further excellent clue to Cypher's nature can be gleaned from his name – in the Robert de Niro film *Angel Heart* (Alan Parker, 1987), the mysterious villain of the piece goes by the name Louis Cypher, which (spoiler warning!) is a Baldrick-quality cunning plan by the Devil himself to hide his true identity. Louis Cypher – Lucifer – geddit? So not only does Cypher represent Judas's betrayal of Jesus, he also provides an obvious satanic reference. Added to this, the fact that Cypher's facial hair and make-up seem to closely match traditional interpretations of what the Devil looks like, and you tend to reach the conclusion that the *Matrix* heroes only have themselves to blame for not spotting the baddie any sooner...

Merovingian: The Merovingian Kings of the Franks ruled from AD 476 – 751 in the area we now know as France. The first 'Merovingian' King was called Clovis, and he united the western Salian Franks with the Ripurarian Franks before converting his entire kingdom to Christianity in 497. The Merovingian's sphere of influence quickly expanded to include the modern areas of Northern France, the Netherlands, Austria, Northern Germany, Burgundy and Provence by 714. The name 'Merovingian' comes from the name of Clovis's grandfather, who established the dynasty. Now, how does this impact directly on *The Matrix*? Well it's hard not to take into account the current strained relationship between the French and the USA. Even before the recent war on Iraq, many American citizens viewed the French as somewhat arrogant, aloof and superior. Following the breakdown in relations between the USA and France owing to the Iraqi war, perhaps we will soon begin to see the French slowly replacing the English as the standard villains in most Hollywood movies!

Morpheus: In Greek mythology, Morpheus was one of the gods of dreams. His job was to create dreams, because the superior gods desired them to be sent to men. Dreams are of course neither real nor based in reality – could this possibly mean that Morpheus has not been telling the truth to Neo? Has he been supplying Neo with a fantasy of his own making?

The legendary Morpheus was assisted in dream-weaving by several other beings, all of whom were working for the Higher Gods. Icelus created dreams that had all the appearance of reality, Phobetor created alarming and scary dreams, and Phantasus tricked sleepers with strange phenomena. However, perhaps most significant to the *Matrix* films is the name of another god of dreams who worked alongside Morpheus in Greek myth. The other god's name? Oneiros. Take another look at that name – ONE-iros.

Are both Neo and Morpheus responsible for planting false dreams in the minds of the ordinary people of Zion? Or is their role a more straightforward one – to help people to see what are dreams and what is reality? By the end of *The Matrix: Reloaded*, we discover that Morpheus's belief in the prophecy about Neo may be misplaced. Has he in fact been misled himself? Has he been the victim of a higher conspiracy? Has the Matrix itself been using Morpheus? Answers will of course be revealed in the third and final movie...

Nebuchadnezzar: One of the ancient kings of Babylon, Nebuchadnezzar is described as the greatest and most powerful of all of their leaders. He lived from 646 to 562 BC. According to historian Sir H. Rawlinson, Nebuchadnezzar 'must have possessed an enormous command of human labour, nine-tenths of Babylon itself, and nineteen-twentieths of all the other ruins that in almost countless profusion cover the land, are composed of bricks stamped with his name. He appears to have built or restored almost every city and temple in the whole country. His inscriptions give an elaborate account of the immense works which he constructed in and about Babylon itself, abundantly illustrating the boast, "Is not this great Babylon which I have built?"' In short, this king was responsible for the rebuilding of his ancient kingdom, and as such it's a worthy name for a ship of freedom fighters. The ancient kingdom of Babylon and the cities that Nebuchadnezzar was responsible for rebuilding are now to be found in the modern state of Iraq – mostly around the city of Baghdad.

> **Neo:** So: Neo means 'new', or 'a new and different form', and comes from the same root as the word 'birth' in French. It's also attached to other words to create a 'modern version' – for instance, 'neo-classical' means 'new classical'. Neo is a particularly suitable nickname for Thomas Anderson to adopt for his hacker persona. Not only does it bring an implication that what he is doing is new, fresh and challenging to the establishment and its status quo, it also brings the weight of classicism and history. In short, it's one heck of a powerful nickname for a computer hacker to have!

Even Neo's 'real' name – Thomas Anderson – has a much deeper meaning than may first appear. Anderson as a name originally derived from the Greek root andr-, meaning 'man'. Therefore, Neo could well be described as being the 'Son of Man' – precisely the phrase used in Christianity to describe Jesus Christ Himself. There are a number of times that Neo is referred to by other characters as their 'personal Jesus Christ', or very similar phrases. Thomas is another intriguing name. It literally means 'companion', someone who travels with you on a journey. As viewers, it's Neo's journey of self-discovery that we tag along with in the *Matrix* films. The name Thomas is also the Greek form of the Aramaic name *Te'oma* which meant 'twin'. In the New Testament, Thomas was the apostle who doubted the resurrected Jesus, creating the expression 'Doubting Thomas'. Neo of course doubts that he is in fact The One, refusing to have faith in his destiny until proof of the prophecy and his involvement in it are shown to him.

Finally, and perhaps most tellingly – Neo is an anagram of One... *The* One.

Niobe: In *The Matrix*, she's a determined and dedicated woman who pilots one of the ships used by the freedom fighters of Zion to resist the control of the Matrix. In legend, Niobe was a figure beset by tragedy. Niobe was a mortal woman who foolishly liked to boast that she had been able to have more children than the goddess Leto. When Leto and the other gods heard of Niobe's arrogance, they took terrible vengeance by killing Niobe's children and then transforming her into a weeping statue. As Niobe in *The Matrix* views the people of Zion as her 'children', does this mean that her actions may cause the death of both herself and some of the other characters? Or perhaps, will her actions in *The Matrix: Revolutions* bring about still greater threats to the last survivors of humanity? Further still, will Niobe's former relationship with Morpheus come back to haunt either of them?

Oracle: In *The Matrix*, the Oracle is an elderly priestess who can predict the future. In perhaps the clearest parallel with legend, the

Oracle receives visions of the future and is visited by people who want to discover what Fate holds for them. In Greek history, the most famous Oracle was a temple at Delphi dedicated to the god Apollo and home to a priestess called the Pythia. She responded to the questions of visitors while in a trance – her inarticulate cries were 'interpreted' by an official spokesperson and then written down. The Pythia's prophecies were notorious for being vague – in many cases, people were only able to deduce the accuracy of her prophecies after the event concerned had taken place! Ancient Greek kings and generals would never become involved in any major campaign or make any significant decisions without first consulting the Pythia to discover if their plans were going to succeed. Interestingly, the Pythia sat on Apollo's tripod to deliver her predictions of the future – in *The Matrix*, the Oracle is seen sitting on a three-legged stool. Even the inscription above the entrance to the Oracle's room is the same as that carved at the entrance of the temple at Delphi – 'Know Thyself'.

Osiris: In *The Matrix*, the *Osiris* is a sister ship to the *Nebuchadnezzar*, captained by Thadeus and populated by a doomed crew of rather attractive CGI characters. In Egyptian legend, Osiris was the God of the Underworld. The oldest Egyptian texts known to scholars refer to him as the great god of the dead – a god who once possessed human form and lived upon the earth. Unlike most ordinary people, Osiris was able to bestow a new life on himself after death – as such an unusual individual, he established himself as the king of a new region into which he admitted everyone who had lived a good and correct life. People who worshipped Osiris were able to follow him into the afterlife – provided they were buried with the correct ceremonies, amulets, spells and rituals.

Osiris was a very highly respected god, being as important to the dead as Ra, the chief Egyptian god, was to the living. He was so important that in some ancient texts Osiris is referred to simply as 'God' rather than by a specific name – a highly important distinction in a culture that worshipped multiple gods. In an unusual link to Persephone, Osiris was the Egyptian god of agriculture and fertility. His death and resurrection were seen as symbolic of the annual harvest and replanting of crops following the regular flooding of the Nile. As such, naming a doomed ship after Osiris has many important resonances. Although the crew of the *Osiris* themselves suffer a brutal death at the hands of the Sentinels, they are able to offer hope for life and rebirth to the people of Zion thanks to the message left in the Matrix by Jue...

Persephone: In Greek mythology, Persephone was the goddess of fertility, harvests and new life. She is also known as Kore ('the maiden'), or the goddess of the budding grain. Persephone was the daughter of Zeus, king of the Gods, and Demeter, the goddess of horticulture. When Persephone was abducted by Hades, god of the underworld, Demeter abandoned her job of keeping the world fertile and the crops growing. As a result, the springs of fertility ran dry – vegetation died off and both men and animals began to expire. Zeus eventually intervened and managed to arrange things so that Persephone would spend half of the year in the underworld with her husband Hades (the Winter) and the rest of the year with her mother Demeter (the Summer), when she would be able to help the world to become a more fertile and enriched place. In *The Matrix: Reloaded*, it appears that Persephone is being held in a 'kept marriage' with her husband, the Merovingian. Although accepting of her duty, it seems that Persephone is not entirely happy with her lot in life. Indeed, she seems to be split between the relationship she has with her sullen husband and her desire for more freedom, represented by her attempt to be passionate with Neo.

Seraph: In Hebrew, a seraph was an angel – hence 'the cherubim and seraphim' of a hundred different Christmas carols – but will Seraph be an angel of good or an angel of death? The extremely wealthy may even own a Seraph of their own – Rolls Royce cars manufacture the Silver Seraph brand. As one of the protectors and guardians of the Oracle, will Seraph have more to do in *The Matrix: Revolutions*?

Tank and Dozer: It's quite ironic that for two 'natural-born' humans, the names they have been given are those of two huge destructive pieces of machinery. Perhaps, rather like the way in which minority groups have sometimes been known to 'reclaim' words that were previously used against them in an offensive manner (e.g. the gay rights movement happily proclaiming 'we're here, we're queer!'), natural-born humans adopt mechanical names. By subverting these names, they become able to make a political statement against their oppressors.

Thadeus: As the captain of the doomed ship, the *Osiris*, Thadeus is the last hope for humanity. When he discovers that the machines are making a final concerted attempt to destroy Zion, Thadeus and his crew make a desperate attempt to hold off the ferocious Sentinels long enough to enable a warning message to be sent to the surviving humans in Zion. So as a last hope for what seems to be a lost cause, it's especially intriguing to discover that one of the early Christian Saints was St Jude Thaddeus. St Jude Thaddeus was distantly related to Christ and was one of the twelve Apostles – the original followers who were with Christ at the last supper before His Crucifixion. At the last supper, Jude asked Christ why he wouldn't be able to manifest Himself to the entire world after His resurrection. Later in his life, Jude wrote a letter (epistle) to Christians in the East in which he preached that the faithful should persevere in harsh, difficult circumstances. Eventually he was martyred in Armenia. Because of his great faith and his ability to cope under extreme pressure, St Jude Thaddeus became the patron saint of desperate cases (or 'hopeless causes') and celebrates his feast day on 28 October each year. Thaddeus also literally means 'the gracious', someone with grace – which definitely applies to the balletic sword-fight we see Thadeus take part in!

Trinity: The word 'trinity' is one of the most important elements of Christian faith. Devout Christians believe that God is simultaneously three persons: the *Father*, the *Son*, and the *Holy Spirit*. Essentially, they believe that all three elements of the One God are part of a single unit. St Maximos the Confessor once wrote: 'The soul has three powers: the intelligence, the incensive power and desire. With our intelligence we direct our search; with our desire we long for the supernal goodness which is the object of our search; and with our incensive power we fight to attain our object.'

So does this mean that Trinity represents the three core values that are needed to successfully achieve a goal – intelligence, desire and power? At the very least, Trinity's name implies holiness, a special purpose and a divine destiny. Following Trinity's death and resurrection at the end of *The Matrix: Reloaded*, what are we to assume? Did Trinity, like Jesus, die and rise from the dead to save humanity? If so, can we expect Trinity to assume some kind of third, higher form in *The Matrix: Revolutions*?

Zion: The name Zion has a number of different meanings in myth, legend and historical fact. Originally it was a stronghold captured by David, the second King of the Israelites. Above it was constructed a temple, and later the name Zion extended to refer to the whole hill. Eventually, the name Zion became interchangeable with the entire city of Jerusalem. In scripture, Zion is also meant to represent an imaginary place believed to be perfect or ideal. So for the last human survivors trying to resist the controlling influence of the Matrix, the name Zion has especially strong connotations – both as a stronghold, and as an idealised place to live. Sadly, as we learn at the conclusion of *The Matrix: Reloaded*, it seems as though Zion may already have fallen to the advance of the machines...

Where do you come from?

| The Philosophy of *The Matrix* |

Philosophers all over the world have spent many years debating the very nature of existence. What is it to be a human being? How do we interact with our fellow humans? How do we know what is real and what isn't real?

One of the first great philosophers of the 'modern' era was René Descartes (1596–1650). Descartes was brought up in Holland and spent much of his early life in preparation for publishing his major works on philosophy. These included *Rules for the Direction of the Mind* (1628), *The World* (1634) and *Discourse on Method* (1637). Descartes's work in philosophy reached its peak with the publications of *Meditations on First Philosophy* (1641) and *Principles of Philosophy* (1644). Much of the philosophical wrangling seen in *The Matrix* films relies heavily upon the work that Descartes was instrumental in founding. Descartes was the first philosopher to ask some very basic questions – concepts that have troubled academics for many years since. In this chapter, I'll attempt to summarise some of the key areas of philosophical debate and highlight how *The Matrix* has brought these concepts to a wide audience.

| Brain in a vat |

The Matrix portrays in a very real and disturbing way one of Descartes's first theories. Descartes argued that as humans, the only things that we actually experience are what our five senses convey through to our brains. A brain simply deals with the information it receives, processes it, and the person comprehends a specific experience – the smell of a flower, the noise of an electric drill, the sight of a firework display. So therefore, apart from the evidence of our senses – which could, of course, be faked – what is there to prove that we actually do exist in a 'real' world at all? Are we able to make any distinction between the brain's interpretation of real things, and fake messages that are piped into the brain? Descartes argues that it is impossible to make that distinction, and that for all we know we could well be living in an entirely illusory world created by some kind of malicious demon or entity (or in the case of *The Matrix*, an evil computer network).

But *The Matrix* goes one little bit further than this. Descartes's most radical theory – which he himself attempted to disprove, but which has been a subject of discussion for philosophers ever since – is one that many people in the real world would have a great deal of difficulty in accepting, but it's the precise reality that Neo finds he's been living in. Descartes postulates that we might never be in direct touch with the real world (if there actually is such a thing as a 'real' world), as we may be being deceived by an evil demon. In modern philosophy, this has come to be known as the 'brain in a vat' hypothesis – if we were merely a brain in a vat being fed information by a computer, how could we possibly know? So when Cypher makes the decision to go back into the Matrix, he's not actually choosing to abandon reality in favour of a fantasy world – if Descartes's hypothesis is accepted, he cannot know that 'reality' exists, and he is therefore simply making a choice between two different fantasies in which to reside.

Descartes's postulation is that all that any of us can directly experience is the content of our own mind, because our mind can only access the external world indirectly – i.e. via our senses, and we know full well that our senses can sometimes deceive us. We've all heard stories of people who have lost limbs in accidents who for months afterwards swear blind that their missing arm or foot is itching like mad. It isn't, because that limb no longer exists – their senses are literally lying to them, telling their brain about something that isn't real. Descartes concluded that for all we know, nothing that we experience might exist at all.

Going back to the hypothesis that we could be just 'brains in vats' (rather than each of us being in possession of a brain inside a cranial vat), a reasonable conclusion is that everything that we 'know' about the world comes from some kind of external stimulus. Let's look at this view from the perspective of the humans plugged into the Matrix. These humans, born inside the machines, are grown in pods and survive in some kind of nutrient slurry. They experience nothing of any 'real' world – these humans do not know how to walk, to talk, what the sky looks like. They know nothing beyond their artificial womb. So how can any of the characters plugged into the Matrix gain the knowledge that they are inside an unreal world? Surely the information supplied to them will prevent them from realising the predicament that they are in?

Well, yes, obviously. In *The Matrix* we discover that it's a combination of the actions of the now-free rebels (giving people a choice of taking the red pill or the blue pill) and the systemic flaws in *The Matrix* programming that allows people like Neo to escape from the 'reality' they are familiar with. Several characters in *The Matrix* universe comment that they begin to fell uneasy about the environment that they have been living in. In the *Animatrix* short 'Kid's Story', the eponymous kid asks the unseen users on his computer network to tell him 'Why it feels more real when I dream than when I'm awake. How can I know if my senses are lying?' In 'World Record', the athlete Dan distorts reality when he pushes himself past the limits of what he knows human beings are capable of achieving. In the 'reality' of the world in which you and I are currently living, there is no helpful pill-pushing Morpheus available to assist us in seeing through the fantasy, nor is there a handily malfunctioning program. If we concede that there is no way of being a hundred per cent certain that the information our brains receive is 'real', then we also have to concede that there is a very real possibility that we are, in fact, just brains floating around in vats being pumped full of information supplied by a different intelligence.

Don't we?

> Nick Bostrom, one of the world's leading science philosophers (who currently works as a Research Fellow at Oxford University), argued in an article for *The Times Higher Education Supplement* ('The Simulation Argument: Why the Probability that You Are Living in a Matrix is Quite High', 16 May 2003) that such a bizarre and frightening concept is not as unlikely as it may first appear. He begins by looking at the technology required to establish a system similar to the one portrayed in *The Matrix* films. Firstly, he points out that most computer scientists believe that the technology will one day exist to create a computer network powerful enough to not only create an entire virtual reality world, but also powerful and versatile enough to simulate millions of different brain patterns. Indeed, many computer scientists believe that it is only a matter of time before it will be possible to transfer the patterns, memories and experiences that are imprinted on a carbon-based computer system (the human brain) on to a silicon-based system: a computer.

It is now possible for scientists to estimate the kind of computing power necessary to create a reasonable facsimile of a human brain along with a virtual reality simulation to provide that brain with an environment in which to live.

Thinking logically, if a civilisation ever came to exist (either on Earth or somewhere else) that was advanced enough to have created the technologies that we dull early-twenty-first-century humans have already worked out can exist, then it is equally valid to assume that such a civilisation would be able to build computers that could handle millions of simulated human brains inside a single virtual-reality program. Therefore there is no scientific reason discovered today why a scenario such as that in *The Matrix* could not exist.

Bostrom then moves on to talk about the specific details of his 'Simulation Argument'. This argument (greatly abbreviated and simplified here!) says the following:

> a) There is the possibility that a civilisation like twenty-first-century Earth will be able to advance to a level of technological expertise where it can create a simulation like *The Matrix*.

b) There is the possibility that some kind of technologically advanced civilisation will want to create computerised simulations of minds like ours.

> c) There is therefore the possibility that you do exist within a simulation.

Bostrom's article is fascinating, and well worth investigating in much greater detail (following the strict rules of propositions within philosophical arguments, of course, rather

than the bastardised version I've presented here).
You can read more here:
http://www.simulation-argument.com/matrix.html

| Simulations and simulacra |

Another important philosophical tract that's worth examining in relation to *The Matrix* was written by the French philosopher Jean Baudrillard in 1981 – *Simulacres et Simulation*. Why is this so important? Well, first of all, Baudrillard's work is all about the erosion of what is real, and how the real has been replaced by simulated images. Baudrillard argues that our 'postmodern' culture is a world where the boundary between the image and the reality is beginning to implode or break down. In particular, he posits that the culture industry blurs the lines between facts, information, entertainment and politics. When the population is bombarded by false images (simulations) and signs (simulacra), they are encouraged to buy products, to vote in a particular way, to work at certain jobs, to aspire to a specific lifestyle.
Eventually, the population will be unable to distinguish between the images that they are presented with and reality, and then they will become apathetic to the difference between the two.
Many current commentators believe that Baudrillard's predictions are becoming ever more pertinent in a society that promotes celebrity for celebrity's sake, and where huge audiences switch on their TV sets to watch a house full of strangers sitting around not doing very much. One particularly

entertaining example of Baudrillard's theory can be found in the very heartland of false images – Disneyland, California. In Disney's new theme park, a new ride has been opened called 'The 405'. The theme park – called 'Disney's California Adventure' – has invented a driving simulation ride, and named it after the freeway on which tourists have to drive to get to the theme park. Adding yet another layer to this postmodern nightmare, the ride features lengthy traffic jams – a notorious problem facing any commuter having to drive along the real 405. So, in short, tourists are now sitting in traffic jams on the 405 Freeway, to pay money to the Disney Corporation, in order to wait in a lengthy queue at the theme park, to sit in a virtual reality simulator of the 405 Freeway, during which they face traffic jams like those they sat in before they arrived at the theme park.

In *The Matrix*, the humans plugged into the system face the ultimate demonstration of Baudrillard's fear – that it's now impossible to see where the simulation or image begins, and where reality ends. And just to ram home the point of how important this particular philosopher is to the Wachowski brothers' vision in *The Matrix*, look again at the sequence near the beginning of the first movie. Thomas Anderson receives a visit from a hacker desperate to get his hands on some important information. He's hidden the goods inside a hollowed-out book – a copy of Jean Baudrillard's *Simulations and Simulacra*.

| 'Real' is a four-letter word |

Morpheus himself tells Neo that everything he experiences is open to being questioned. He says to Neo, 'How do you define real? If you're talking about what you can feel, what you can smell, what you can taste and see – then 'real' is simply electrical signals interpreted by your brain.' So Morpheus seems to be siding with Descartes's world view! However one thing that is not questioned by many viewers of *The Matrix* is the moral judgement that the viewer generally passes on the behaviour of the characters. We are led to believe that what Neo, Morpheus and Trinity are doing is inherently good. Our heroes are fighting to reveal the truth – a noble cause in a society that's still continually questioning whether the official line we are fed by the media, by government, by our employers, is actually the truth. As Fox Mulder in *The X-Files* was constantly searching ('The Truth is Out There'), so the heroes of *The Matrix* will stop at nothing to help to undermine the artificial reality created by the machines, and thereby to free the millions of plugged-in humans. But are they doing the right thing?

The character of Cypher presents us with an interesting dilemma. Like the rest of the heroes, he has been unplugged. He's taken the red pill, and has discovered what the 'real' world is truly like. And he doesn't like it one little bit. Who, in their heart of hearts, can blame Cypher for his hatred of the truth? His life in the real world is as a refugee,

> continually hunted by the lethal machines he's escaped from. There are no pleasures in life for him – they live in a world of vile frogspawn-like food replacement, of drab clothes, dreary claustrophobic living conditions and the constant threat of imminent painful death. So why are we led to automatically condemn Cypher for his decision to betray his colleagues and ask the machines to re-immerse him in *The Matrix*? Putting aside for one moment the inherent moral problems in betraying and murdering your colleagues and the automatic emotional response that such acts bring, is it actually wrong to want what Cypher desires?

Cypher's desire is simply to replace one set of stimuli with another. He's lived in the 'real' world for long enough now that he has come to realise that the things the crew of the *Nebuchadnezzar* are trying to achieve are illusions themselves. He believes that the only ultimate freedom and ultimate reality is to go back into the Matrix – to ascend to a higher state of consciousness within the Matrix itself. Cypher justifies his decision to return to the Matrix in a stinging attack on Morpheus. He tells his former leader that 'if you would have told us the truth, we would've told you to shove that red pill right up your ass'. When Trinity argues that Morpheus has set them free, Cypher counters with a valid point – that all he does now is follow Morpheus's orders, not the Matrix's. So what's the difference?

> Surely if – as Morpheus himself admitted – reality is entirely a matter of perception and the electrical signals being pumped into your brain, then the only matter of morality to be debated is the question of free will, and whether or not it's important to exercise that free will. Even in the supposed 'free world', it becomes ever clearer that the actions of these so-called 'free' people may not be as free as they thought. Neo, in particular, spends much of *The Matrix* and *The Matrix: Reloaded* trying to come to terms with a destiny that's pre-ordained thanks to the Oracle's prophecy. As we later discover, the Oracle her(it?)self is a computer program, so just how much influence does the predictions of a computer program that lives inside the Matrix have on the lives of the 'free' humans? The even more shocking revelation from the Architect – that the Matrix has deliberately led Neo and the other humans into believing in the false prophecy of The One who will free humanity from the control of the machines – just adds further support to Cypher's decision that the reality of the Matrix is just as valid as the reality of the *Nebuchadnezzar*.

By the end of *The Matrix*, Neo appears to have become The One – as predicted by the computer program, the Oracle. His mission, to free the people trapped in the Matrix from slavery, has only just begun. Neo now has the ability to change the laws of reality and physics inside the Matrix, as shown by his 'Superman' flight in the last shot of the movie. However in *The Matrix: Reloaded*, we see no attempts by Neo to use his new-found powers to free the individual humans trapped inside the Matrix itself. As essentially the new Messiah of humanity, Neo seems to be doing very little about it. By the conclusion of *The Matrix: Reloaded*, Neo experiences another surprise. On the surface of the real world, surrounded by the charred and shattered ruins of the former human cities, Neo is able to use his powers as The One to repel a group of Sentinels and save the lives of himself and his friends. Does this mean that finally Neo has begun to become The One? Is he about to transform into a saviour who can combat the machines both inside and outside of the Matrix?

Or is there a far more disturbing possibility? We know that the powers of The One have, until now, only been able to exist within the computer-simulated world of the Matrix. What if the 'real' world of Zion, the *Nebuchadnezzar* and the shattered ruins of human civilisation is itself a computer-generated illusion, a simulation of a simulation, just as Baudrillard argues our modern society is becoming. The answers will of course become clearer in *The Matrix: Revolutions*...

WHAT DO YOU BELIEVE?

| *The Matrix* and religion |

With its policy of borrowing elements from a variety of different religions and moral structures to create a single whole, many viewers have found *The Matrix*'s pot-pourri of themes and perspectives to be quite an attractive amalgam. I wouldn't for one moment begin to suggest which religions (if any) the Wachowski brothers are trying to promote via their films. I'd much rather suggest that what they are doing in their series of films is providing intelligent viewers with a selection of theories and concepts, suggestions of different ways of thinking and looking at the world and our view of 'God', redemption, heaven and all of those really heavy things that most people don't bother with any more in the secular UK. In this chapter, some of the main world religions (including one that was forgotten for nearly 1600 years!) and the key themes that are presented in *The Matrix* films will be examined.

Christianity: Think back for a moment to the moment in *The Matrix* where Neo is engaged in conversation with his new 'friend' Cypher. Neo is trying to come to terms with the realisation that everything that he's ever known in his life has in fact been a computer-generated illusion. Added to this, Morpheus has just told him that he's destined to be The One, the saviour of the humans left trapped within the Matrix and of the rebels fighting back against the machines. Cypher asks Neo: 'Did he tell you why you're here?' It's all Neo can do just to nod. 'Jesus!' replies Cypher. 'What a mindjob. So you're here to save the world?'

Well, actually, Cypher's pretty much correct in everything he says there. To all intents and purposes, Neo is equivalent to Christ. He is there to save the world. And this is a job for Neo's mind – to overcome the fantasy world he's been made to believe in, and to operate on a higher level within the computer simulation of the Matrix.

Throughout all of *The Matrix* films there are continual references to many different kinds of religion. For a Western audience raised in the United Kingdom or the USA, it's perhaps easiest to spot the parallels with Christianity, such as the one mentioned above. Traditional Christian teaching is based around the belief that there is one God, who created the Universe. God decided to populate the world that he created with humans, beings to whom he gave free will – the ability to make moral decisions and judgements of their own. The Christian God therefore only allows people who behave in a morally acceptable way to join him in Heaven following their deaths. In order to show the confused people of the world how to lead a good and decent life – and therefore how to get into Heaven – God sent his son, Jesus Christ, to Earth as humanity's saviour, in order to show them the way. In *The Matrix*, one of the very first people that Neo meets is a fellow computer hacker. Neo hands the hacker a disk full of valuable information. 'Hallelujah!' responds the hacker. 'You're my saviour, man – my own personal Jesus Christ.'

Such links might be dismissed as mere coincidence, were it not for Neo's story throughout the Matrix films, which in several important ways closely parallels Christ's life. Many people are unaware of the fact that Jesus Christ definitely lived as a historical figure. There are many accounts from records taken by the Roman authorities in Judea around the time of AD 30 that detail the activities of a young Jewish leader called Jesus of Nazareth. Jesus was perceived by the authorities as a huge danger to their regime, because he led a group of rebels who began to organise themselves. Even more controversially, these rebels began to try to convert the ordinary citizens, preaching to them that the only way to achieve everlasting peace and happiness was to ask forgiveness from God for their sins. Similarly, Neo becomes a threat to the machines and the Matrix when he joins forces with the other rebels on board the *Nebuchadnezzar* and attempts to destabilise the regime.

For a short while, Neo questions whether or not he is The One. Despite the protestations of Morpheus, Neo refuses to believe that he is in any way important. Perhaps it may have been worth his while to check out the registration plate on the hull of the *Nebuchadnezzar*. The plate details the name of the ship, when it was constructed, and then its serial number – Mark III, No.11. Anyone familiar with the New Testament of the Christian Bible might realise that this is a reference to one of the four Gospels. The Gospels are four distinct books that form the first section of the New Testament. In particular, the Gospels (written by Matthew, Mark, Luke and John) tell the story of Jesus's birth, life and death. As with all books in the Bible, Mark's Gospel is subdivided into chapters and verses. If we look up Mark, Chapter 3, Verse 11 in the Authorised Version, it reads: 'And unclean spirits, when they saw him, fell down before him, and cried, saying, Thou art the Son of God.' So not only does Morpheus reckon that Neo is The One, but his ship does too!

Skipping forward to *The Animatrix*'s 'Final Flight Of The *Osiris*', we note that there's a slightly different nameplate welded to the hull of the *Osiris* – Mark VI, No.16. This verse of Mark's gospel reads: 'But when Herod heard thereof, he said, It is John, whom I beheaded: he is risen from the dead.' This is a reference to Herod Antipas, the Roman-appointed king of the region of Galilee. Herod had been unwillingly responsible for the beheading of the prophet John the Baptist, the man who had foretold the coming of Jesus Christ as Messiah of the Jewish people. So how does this verse of Mark's gospel fit into *The Matrix*? Does it foretell a nasty death for Morpheus (the character most closely linked with John the Baptist)? Or is it just predicting the fate of Thadeus and the crew of the *Osiris* – that despite the machines' belief that they have stopped the threat to their regime, the secret message planted in the Matrix will come back to haunt them.

So what does the Bible say about the birth of Jesus? Thanks to endless Nativity plays in schools, most people know that Jesus's mother was Mary and that his father was Joseph the carpenter. However, the New Testament of the Bible teaches that owing to a miraculous conception Mary was still a virgin when she gave birth to her son – in other words, that Jesus was not created by natural means. Neo, of course, was grown by the machines inside a giant vat of nutrient chemicals – like Jesus, he was not the result of union between man and woman. While Jesus was growing up, there was a prophet, somebody preparing the way for his arrival by preaching that the saviour would soon be there. In the Bible, this is John the Baptist – in *The Matrix*, it's Morpheus. When Jesus was ready to begin his teachings, he met John the Baptist and underwent a baptism of his own. In *The Matrix* it's the job of Morpheus and the rest of the crew of the *Nebuchadnezzar* to 'baptise' Neo as they give him the red pill and induce his rebirth into the tank of slurry.

> The Bible tells the story of how Jesus spends forty days in the desert preparing for the final stages of his life. At that moment, the Devil appears to Jesus and tempts him with riches, happiness and dominion over the world – provided that he turns away from his pre-ordained path (Luke 4: 1–13). Similarly, the Agents do their best to get Neo to betray his friends.

Undoubtedly for Christians the most important part in the story of Jesus is his sacrifice and resurrection from the dead. Christians believe that Jesus willingly allowed himself to be crucified by the Roman authorities – a particularly lengthy and painful death – so that through the act of sacrifice all of his followers would be able to gain access to heaven. In short, as it says in Mark 10: 45, 'even the Son of Man came not to be ministered unto, but to minister and to give his life in ransom for many' . In the first *Matrix* film, Neo consciously makes the decision to sacrifice his life in order to save Morpheus – but by this very act, Neo enables the prophecy foretold by the Oracle to be fulfilled.

Neo dies, killed by the bullets fired from an Agent's gun. Neo knew that this was coming – the Oracle had foretold that either he or Morpheus would die. In addition, the Oracle had told Neo that he wasn't The One, and that he was waiting for something – 'maybe your next life'. When Jesus died, executed by the Romans, his body was resurrected, brought back from the dead by God. In *The Matrix*, Neo is brought back to life by another power – a kiss from Trinity. It's easy to forget, however, that the Christian God is often described as being three beings in one – a Holy Trinity (for more info, see **'What's In A Name'**). The resurrected Jesus was not just a 'normal' human being – his resurrected body was not bound by the same rules that governed ordinary mortals. Similarly, Neo possesses abilities that far exceed those of his colleagues – he's super-fast, able to dodge any physical threats that the Agents may throw at him. Jesus's last act on Earth was to

> physically ascend into Heaven to join God, his Father. And of course, the final shot of *The Matrix* sees Neo literally shooting up into the heavens (although in a pose that owes more to the Son of Jor-El than to the Son of God).

By the time we get to see what has happened to the characters in *The Matrix: Reloaded*, events have moved on significantly. Neo is now being accepted as a possible saviour by more than just the crew of the *Nebuchadnezzar* – in fact, more or less the entire population of Zion, all 250,000 free humans, have placed some degree of faith in him and his ability to save them from the rule of the machines. Furthermore, Neo's new religion – that of being able to stand up against the rule of an oppressive regime – follows closely the way in which Christianity spread throughout the Roman Empire in the early centuries BC. Possibly we will see a parallel in *The Matrix: Revolutions*, whereby some of the machines become converted to Neo's way of thinking, and eventually the regime is overthrown from within...

Gnostisism: One of the most intriguing elements to the Matrix films is their heavy reliance upon religious imagery, plotlines, characters and concepts. For a modern viewer, many of these concepts may be unfamiliar – I've spent more than a little time explaining to my younger relatives exactly what the Christian concept of the Holy Trinity is. As the in-depth study of traditional Christianity wanes in State schools in the United Kingdom, it's more likely than ever before that certain concepts will need to be explained.

However, despite the use of many elements of Christian teaching, philosophy and morality in the films, *The Matrix* is not at heart a 'Christian' tale. Because the films take elements from a large variety of different faiths, belief systems and traditions, the best word to use to describe the Wachowskis' work is syncretistic. One of the key religions that *The Matrix* fuses into its whole is one that for many centuries was lost – Gnosticism. Named after the Greek word 'gnosis' (or 'knowledge'), Gnostics have a very different perspective to followers of most other religions, one that is mirrored in the actions of Neo in the *Matrix* films. In short, Neo becomes a similar figure in *The Matrix* to the Messiah in Gnostic teachings – the character who arrives in a world to show the other inhabitants the truth about the reality in which they find themselves. In order to understand this perspective more fully, it's useful to unearth more about the history of Gnosticism.

Throughout the second century, several Christian writers (such as Justin Martyr and Iranaeus) preached to their followers about a dangerous new faith called Gnosticism. They told the readers of their letters that Gnosticism was heretical to the true faith – if you followed the teachings of the Gnostics, then you would be damned to hell. Up until the middle of the twentieth century, though, nobody knew exactly what the Gnostics had been teaching, because the early Christians had done a particularly effective job in erasing it from history. Then in 1945 a man called Muhammad Ali (no, not the boxer!) found a jar buried near the town of Nag Hammadi, Egypt. Inside the jar were thirteen leather-bound books, which after some intense scientific research were found to date from c. AD 350. These books contained almost intact versions of many of the early Gnostic texts – including their interpretation of the story of Jesus Christ's life on Earth. These texts were finally translated into English in 1977, sparking a frenzy of activity from theological academics around the world. So what do the Gnostic texts actually teach?

> The core belief of the Gnostic gospel starts with the argument that the world in which we live is inherently not a good place and that it was not created by a supreme, all-powerful and benevolent god or gods. On this basis alone, it therefore contradicts hugely the beliefs of almost all other organised religions across the globe. In fact, Gnostics argue that the world was created by a lesser god, one that didn't have the ability or skills to create a perfect world that would last forever. This world in which we live is therefore imperfect – replete with pain, sorrow and death, and full of beings that long to be released from this existence of flesh and blood. However, deep within each being on the planet is a

spark that links humans with the supreme being that created the whole of the Universe, a being that nobody can see or contact. The only way for humanity to contact this god is to evolve beyond its current flesh and blood state and achieve 'perfection'. Gnostics argue that Jesus descended from Heaven for a very specific reason – not to 'die for our sins' as most Christians believe, but to show humanity the way to ascend to self-perfection.

The most influential of the Gnostic writers (from what we can glean from the thirteen texts discovered in Egypt) was Valentinus, who wrote in Rome c. AD 140. He combined the concepts of the earliest books of the New Testament with the thinking that was prevalent amongst leading Greek thinkers. Valentinus's interpretation of Gnosticism follows many of the core concepts found in the other, non-Valentinus-scribed texts found in the jar – essentially, that 'something is wrong with the world', and that it's the fault of the being that created that world rather than the fault of the person experiencing it. Valentinus teaches that the whole of creation came into existence thanks to a being called Bythos. Bythos 'expelled' thirty beings called aeons (or pleroma) from itself. One of the more lowly of these aeons was named Wisdom, or Sophia. She became pregnant (are you keeping up with all of this?!) and gave birth to Jehovah, the god who in turn created the physical world as we know it. Valentinus argued that as Jehovah wasn't the supreme being, the world that he created was imperfect – 'wrong', in some way. Valentinus's view on how mankind can achieve redemption or salvation has a great deal more in common with Hinduism and Buddhism than, say, orthodox Christianity. Jesus is an important figure to Gnostics not because he is the Son of God, but rather because of the information he holds. In *The Matrix*, Neo is The One, not because he is born special, a god, or any form of superior being. No, he is The One because of the information he holds – that he is different, that he knows how to see through the unreality that is presented around him. Indeed, in the few point-of-view shots we get from Neo's perspective, we note how he can now literally see the code that binds the Matrix together – the strings of green figures that cascade around him. Neo is The One because he sees and knows more than the other characters do. He can see that the world is wrong, and that knowledge gives him the power to change that world.

For further reading on Gnosticism and how *The Matrix* is influenced by its teachings, you may want to go here: www.gnosis.org/

Buddhism: In Zen Buddhism, one of the most crucial lessons to learn is the importance of being able to have a clear image of oneself, to have a clear or 'mirror' mind. With a mind uncluttered by the everyday rubbish of human life, it becomes possible to see yourself as you do in a mirror – to see yourself as you truly are. Throughout the early parts of *The Matrix*, there are repeated mirror images of Thomas Anderson, as he slowly begins to realise who he is and the fact that the world he knows isn't real. From the window cleaners in Mr Rhinehart's office wiping away the soap suds (which look suspiciously like the green digital code of the Matrix itself), through to the reflections in Morpheus's sunglasses; each time, Thomas Anderson gets closer and closer to discovering his true reflection – that he is in fact Neo. As soon as Neo swallows the red pill, the mirror he stands next to seems to swallow and absorb him entirely.

The clearest use of Buddhist teaching in *The Matrix* appears during the famously puzzling 'spoon-bending' sequence inside the Oracle's apartment. The spoon-bending boy is dressed as a Buddhist monk, and sits in a full lotus position – synonymous with Buddhist prayer. When the boy informs Neo that there 'is no spoon', Neo is confused – clearly, there is a spoon there. For one thing, he can see his own reflection in it! The relevance of this scene becomes clear when one considers a well-known Buddhist parable. In the parable, three monks are

> talking about a flag that they can see blowing in the wind. The first monk observes how the flag seems to be moving. The second one replies by saying that it's not the flag that's moving, but the wind that moves about and the flag simply reacts to the wind – it doesn't move of its own accord. The third monk then tells the other two off – it's not the flag, nor the wind that moves, but their minds.

The parallel with the spoon-bending boy's comment is clear… everything that Neo is seeing inside the Matrix is all in his mind. There is no spoon – only the images that he can see within the Matrix.

RED PILL

100
100
100
001
000
101
010
100
110
100
001
100
100
101
000
010
100
001
011
000
010
110
101
000
101
011
101
001
001
010
101
010
101
001
001
011
001
001
000
010
001
010
101
001
101
000

So you want to take the Red Pill? Be sure. Be very sure. Even now it is not too late to turn back. Because once you've taken the Red Pill, your perception of what is real and what isn't real will never be the same again. You'll discover some unpleasant truths that you might wish you'd never uncovered. You'll be forced to look closely at who you are, why you've made the choices you've made up until now, and most importantly you'll discover where the real control lies. Ready? 'Cause Kansas is about to go bye-bye…

WHAT IS THE MATRIX?

In the spirit of today's fast-food society, here's a selection of the very best pick'n'mix facts and figures about *The Matrix* movies in an easily digestible, txt msg style. There's a lot to get through here, so eyes down and pay attention at the back…

♦ Original casting choices for the role of Neo included Ewan McGregor (who turned it down as he was busy making *Star Wars: Episode I – The Phantom Menace*) and Will Smith (declined in favour of *Wild Wild West*). Val Kilmer was seriously considered for the role of Morpheus.

♦ The principal cast spent from October 1997 through to March 1998 learning an assortment of martial arts so that they would be able to withstand the rigours of filming the fight scenes in *The Matrix*.

♦ Carrie Anne Moss badly twisted her ankle during one of the first scenes she filmed as Trinity but decided not to tell anyone in case they decided to recast her.

♦ Many different people may lay claim to having invented the photographic technique showcased in *The Matrix* in the famous 'bullet-time' sequence. The process essentially involves placing a circle of still cameras around the person or object to be photographed, then triggering each of the cameras simultaneously. By playing these images back in a traditional projector, the camera seems to move smoothly around an object that's frozen in time. Graphic artist Matthew Bannister, artist Tim Macmillan and video director Michel Gondry all appear to have developed near-identical techniques in the early 1990s, but it was undoubtedly its use in *The Matrix* that established this process as a favourite of special effects artists and advertisers throughout the world.

♦ Some people have suggested that the 'real' name of the traitorous Cypher – Reagan – is a cheap jibe at the former President of the United States, currently suffering from Alzheimer's Disease. Personally, I don't know what they're talking about: when Cypher confesses that he wants to be 'someone important', 'an actor' and 'remember nothing', I'm sure it's just a terrible coincidence...

♦ In the artificial-reality world of *The Matrix*, there are many directions given to street corners such as Wells and Lake. In reality, all of these streets exist in the Wachowski Brothers' hometown of Chicago.

♦ Thomas Anderson works for a software company called Metacortex, a name derived from the Latin for beyond or outside the brain.

♦ Principal photography on *The Matrix* (the sequences where the main cast are involved, as opposed to any later work on special-effects shots, for instance) took 118 days, between March and August 1998. The final sequence shot was of the escape attempt through the dry-wall.

♦ The budget for the production of *The Matrix* came in at a relatively modest $63 million, significantly lower than for many of the other blockbuster action films made in the same year.

♦ All of the city locations in *The Matrix* were shot in Sydney, Australia, as it was a much more cost-effective option than recording in Los Angeles or another city in the USA. As Sydney is such a modern, clean city, many of the run-down back alleys and city streets had to be either 'dirtied' on location or recreated later in the studio.

♦ During its initial run in cinemas, *The Matrix* clocked up an impressive box-office take of £17 million in the UK, $171m in the USA, and a further $203m around the rest of the world.

♦ When the first trailer for *The Matrix: Reloaded* was made available online, it was downloaded two million times in the first 72 hours.

♦ Filming of *The Matrix: Reloaded* was hit by two untimely deaths. Singer/actress Aaliyah died in a plane crash prior to recording her scenes as Zee, and Gloria Foster (The Oracle) died of complications relating to her diabetes after completing work on *Reloaded* but prior to commencing filming the scripted scenes for *The Matrix: Revolutions*.

♦ The two sequels were in production for an epic 270 days of principal photography.

♦ The 17-minute motorway chase sequence cost $40 million to shoot and took 45 days to complete. As it would have been impossible to shut down a genuine American freeway for lengthy periods in order to shoot the necessary action sequences, a replica freeway was constructed in its entirety on the Alameda Point Navy Base in

California. The replica freeway ran for 1.4 miles and was demolished when filming was complete. General Motors donated some 300 cars for use in the production of this sequence, many of which were wrecked beyond repair.

♦ The two freeways mentioned during the chase sequence are the 101 and the 303, which by a staggering coincidence are the numbers of Thomas Anderson's apartment and the room Trinity is discovered in during the opening of *The Matrix* respectively. The exits from the 101 freeway that are given name checks during the chase are also genuine exits from the real-life 101 freeway in California.

♦ Carrie Anne Moss went one better on filming *The Matrix* sequels. Having badly twisted her ankle on the first film, she ended up breaking her leg entirely while training for the extensive amount of wire-work that would be required in the movies.

♦ When the Wachowski Brothers signed their contracts to make both sequels, there was a specific clause written in that stipulated they would not have to do any publicity for the sequels whatsoever.

♦ There are more than 2000 special-effects shots in the two *Matrix* sequels – in the first film, there were 400.

♦ Keanu Reeves received a salary of $10 million for *The Matrix*. His estimated salary for the two sequels, based around a percentage of the overall box-office takings, will probably exceed $50 million.

♦ The budget for the two *Matrix* sequels was a combined $237 million, with $127 million of that total being spent on *Reloaded*.

♦ Aside from the replica freeway and some sequences shot in the Californian city of Oakland, all of the two sequels were once again filmed in Australia in order to save costs. The studios used on all three films were the Fox Studios, Sydney.

♦ During the 'burly brawl' sequence between Neo and the numerous Agent Smiths, up to a dozen stuntmen stood in for Hugo Weaving and had to have their heads shaved prior to replica toupees being fitted in order to match Weaving's own thinning thatch.

♦ To date, *The Matrix: Reloaded* has taken £31 million at the UK box office (a huge increase on *The Matrix*'s take). This increase in revenue has been matched in the USA ($269 million at time of going to press) and in other markets around the world ($250m to date).

WHO ARE YOU?

One of the most annoying things that can happen when you're watching a film or a TV show is when you see somebody on screen and you go, 'ooh, where have I seen that person before?' By the time you've wracked your brains for the information, asked everyone who you're sitting with and then still not come up with the goods, you've missed an important bit of the plot and you're more confused than before.

Well worry no more! In this chapter, you can find out what projects the talented people behind *The Matrix* films have been involved with before. Use these pages as a guide to discovering new films and TV shows that you may not have thought about watching before – and of course ones to avoid like the plague!

| Crew |

Andy and Larry Wachowski

(Writers, Directors, Producers): The Wachowski Brothers, Andy (born 29 December 1967) and Larry (born 21 June 1965), were responsible for just two other film projects before *The Matrix* began to dominate their lives. In 1995 they scripted *Assassins*, an action-adventure that starred Sylvester Stallone and Antonio Banderas. The following year they wrote, directed and produced *Bound*, the lesbi-chic heist movie that paired off Jennifer Tilly and Gina Gershon (and also featured future *Matrix* star Joe Pantoliano as Gershon's cuckolded mobster boyfriend). Featuring many of the directorial flourishes that signify *The Matrix*, *Bound* is a roller-coaster ride of a thriller with a plot containing more twists and turns than a bowl full of spaghetti. Definitely worth watching for any *Matrix* fan who loves a thriller with a brain. And no, I'm not going to mention the lesbian love scenes. Oh, no siree.

Joel Silver

(Producer): Joel Silver is now almost as legendary in Hollywood as the films he has produced. The consummate publicist is a larger-than-life character who often acts as a one-man publicity machine for his own projects. Born in New Jersey on 14 July 1952, Silver's first job as producer was in the gang drama *The Warriors* (Walter Hill, 1979). Moving swiftly onto a far more glamorous project, Silver co-produced the legendarily naff Olivia Newton-John musical

Xanadu (Robert Greenwald, 1982) before getting his first mainstream success with the Nick Nolte/Eddie Murphy comedy-thriller *48 Hours* (Walter Hill, 1982). Throughout the 1980s, Silver was responsible for many of the highest-profile and most popular Hollywood movies, including *Brewster's Millions* (Walter Hill, 1985), *Commando* (Mark L. Lester, 1985), and Whoopi Goldberg's comedy *Jumpin' Jack Flash* (Penny Marshall, 1986).

In 1987, Silver produced an action movie with a relatively small budget and two relatively unknown stars, that would become synonymous with the action genre. The stars were Mel Gibson and Danny Glover, and the film was the original *Lethal Weapon* (Richard Donner, 1987). Spoting a genre where his skills found their natural home, Silver went on to produce a steady stream of blockbuster action movies, including *Predator* (John McTiernan, 1987), *Die Hard* (John McTiernan, 1988), and many sequels to his *Lethal Weapon/Die Hard/Predator* franchises.

After a brief lull in the mid 1990s when several of Silver's projects seemed to lack the box-office magic of his earlier work, he began work with two relatively unknown directors called the Wachowski Brothers on a science-fiction action movie called *The Matrix*. Silver's work on the three *Matrix* films has re-established him as one of Hollywood's major players. He's surely a face to keep a very close tab on in the future.

Don Davis

(Composer): Don Davis (born 4 February 1957) has written the music scores for more than 70 different projects and orchestrated half as many again. His work on TV shows such as *Hart to Hart*, *Beauty and the Beast* and *Star Trek: The Next Generation* complements his film work, which includes the Wachowski Brothers' *Bound* (1996), *Jurassic Park III* (Joe Johnston, 2001), *Behind Enemy Lines* (John Moore, 2001) and, of course, *The Matrix* trilogy.

Bill Pope

(Cinematographer): The Cinematographer on any movie is responsible for the overall 'look' of the film – in particular, for ensuring that each frame of the film looks as beautiful as possible. Aside from *The Matrix* films, Bill Pope has 'lensed' *Darkman* (1990), *Army Of Darkness: Evil Dead III* (1993) and *Spider-Man II* (2004) (AKA *The Amazing Spiderman*) all for the legendary horror and fantasy director Sam Raimi. He brought his unique touch to the Wachowskis' first movie *Bound* (1996) and the box-office hits *Gridlock'd* (Vondie Curtis-Hall, 1997) and *Bedazzled* (Harold Ramis, 2000).

John Gaeta

(Visual Effects): Born in 1965, John Gaeta had worked in a junior capacity on the visual effects for *Judge Dredd* (Danny Cannon, 1995) and *Eraser* (Chuck Russell, 1996) before landing his first job as Visual Effects Supervisor on *The Matrix*, a role he's repeated in both *Matrix: Reloaded* and *Matrix: Revolutions*.

Kym Barrett

(Costume Design): The very talented Kym Barrett had worked on movies such as Baz Luhrmann's *Romeo + Juliet* (1996) and *Zero Effect* (Jake Kasdan, 1988) before getting the job of creating the costumes for *The Matrix*. She then went on to work on science fiction flicks *Titan A.E.* (Don Bluth, 2000) – for which she designed the costumes for the animated characters to 'wear' – and *Red Planet* (Anthony Hoffman, 2000). She then travelled back in time to work on the Jack the Ripper thriller *From Hell* (The Hughes Brothers, 2001) before returning to work on the two *Matrix* sequels.

| Cast |

Keanu Reeves

(Thomas Anderson / Neo): Keanu Charles Reeves was born on 2 September 1964 in the soon-to-be war-torn city of Beirut, Lebanon. Keanu, which means 'cool breeze over the mountains' in Hawaiian (!) was also the name of his great-great uncle. At school he was nicknamed 'The Wall' because he was an extremely good defender when playing ice hockey. Reeves dropped out of school to make his name as an actor, spending much of the early part of his career appearing in TV movies and untransmitted pilots (sometimes under the names Norman Kreeves, K.C. Reeves or Chuck Spidena). Reeves made his first significant big-screen appearance in *Youngblood* (Peter Markle, 1986), the Rob Lowe-starring ice-hockey flick. Reeves then went on to chalk up a number of supporting roles in films such as *River's Edge* (Tim Hunter, 1986), *The Night Before* (Thom Eberhardt, 1988), *Permanent Record* (Marisa Silver, 1988) and *The Prince Of Pennsylvania* (Ron Nyswaner, 1988). In 1989, he got his first real taste of stardom, playing the boyfriend/husband of Martha Plimpton in *Parenthood* (Ron Howard, 1989). But it was as vacuous LA high-school student Ted 'Theodore' Logan that Reeves really connected with an audience. *Bill & Ted's Excellent Adventure* (Stephen Herek, 1989) became a cult classic that spawned an animated spin-off series and a sequel – *Bill & Ted's Bogus Journey* (Peter Hewitt, 1991), for which Reeves and his co-star Alex Winter returned to play both their original characters and their evil counterparts, 'Evil Bill' and 'Evil Ted'. As Ted, Keanu created a cultural icon whose impact would stand the test of time – indeed, even in *The Matrix* itself, the audience knew exactly what the Wachowski Brothers were getting at when they allowed Neo to gasp 'Whoa!' In fact, the first time I saw *The Matrix* in the cinema, several members of the audience shouted out 'Dude!', completing the famous catchphrase from the *Bill & Ted* films.

Though he would continue to play 'drop-out types' in films such as *I Love You To Death* (Lawrence Kasdan, 1990), in *My Own Private Idaho* (Gus Van Sant, 1991), he took on a role that provided him with more of a challenge. Reeves played Scott, a rent boy on a quest to track down his mother. Switching genres completely, Reeves then began to position himself as an attractive action hero in films like *Point Break* (Kathryn Bigelow, 1991), opposite Patrick Swayze, *Speed* (Jan de Bont, 1994), with Sandra Bullock, and *Chain Reaction* (Andrew Davis, 1996). He also took on literary adaptations and art-house projects that challenged both public perceptions – such as in *Little Buddha* (Bernardo Bertolucci, 1993) – and his (not entirely successful) ability to pull off an English accent in *Bram Stoker's Dracula* (Francis Ford Coppola, 1992) and *Much Ado About Nothing* (Kenneth Branagh, 1993).

Though Reeves rarely plays slackers any more, and his body might be slightly more 'buff' than that of the gangly youth he once was, he still struggles to rid himself completely of the misty-eyed bafflement that runs through many of his characters. In recent years, *Johnny Mnemonic* (Robert Longo,

1995), *A Walk In The Clouds* (Alfonso Arau, 1995) and *The Devil's Advocate* (Taylor Hackford, 1997) have played upon the wide-eyed innocence that is undoubtedly Reeve's main appeal to his fans.

Reeves is currently working on three new movies, to be released in 2003 and 2004, including an intriguing-sounding sci-fi thriller called *Constantine* (directed by Francis Lawrence).

Laurence Fishburne

(Morpheus): Early on in his acting career, Laurence Fishburne (born 30 July 1961 in Atlanta, Georgia) was known as 'Larry'. His first major role was as 'Clean', one of the boat crew accompanying Martin Sheen in Francis Ford Coppola's *Apocalypse Now* (1979). He worked with Coppola again on *Rumble Fish* (1983), *The Cotton Club* (1984) and *Gardens Of Stone* (1987). Other major film projects as 'Larry Fishburne' include *The Color Purple* (Steven Spielberg, 1985), *School Daze* (Spike Lee, 1986), *King Of New York* (Abel Ferrara, 1990), *Boyz N The Hood* (John Singleton, 1991) and *Deep Cover* (Bill Duke, 1992). To play legendary soul singer Ike Turner in *What's Love Got To Do With It* (Brian Gibson, 1993) – for which he received an Academy Award nomination – Fishburne adopted the more formal 'Laurence', which he's kept ever since.

Since then, Laurence has portrayed Shakespeare's *Othello* (Oliver Parker, 1995) opposite Kenneth Branagh's villainous Iago, has ventured into space in the truly abysmal science-fiction shocker *Event Horizon* (Paul Anderson, 1997), and has even been the voice of cartoon character Thrax in *Osmosis Jones* (Bobby and Peter Farrelly, 2001). Since completing work on *The Matrix* sequels, Laurence has been directing a new movie called *The Alchemist*, due for release in 2004. Laurence split from his first wife Hajna Moss in the late 1990s – together they have two children, Langston and Montana. Laurence is married to actress Gina Torres, who of course has a small role in *The Matrix: Reloaded* as Cas, the widow of Tank.

Carrie-Anne Moss

(Trinity): Former model Carrie-Anne Moss is Canadian, born 21 August 1967 in Vancouver. She first hit the small screen as Tara McDonald in the American TV series *Dark Justice* (which for its first season was filmed on location in Barcelona). Entirely coincidentally, she next worked on a TV show called *Matrix* (which starred Nick Mancuso as a hitman) among a number of other small TV roles. These included stretches on shows as diverse as *Models Inc*, *F/X The Series* and even the 1990s *Spider-Man* animated series, for which she provided many of the additional voices. Good groundwork for her guest appearances in *The Animatrix*!

Her breakthrough film, *The Matrix*, catapulted her into the big league; she followed up the sci-fi smash with appearances in the brain-addling thriller *Memento* (Christopher Nolan, 2000), sci-fi caper *Red Planet* (Anthony Hoffman, 2000) and *Chocolat* (Lasse Halström, 2000) before rejoining *The Matrix* cast for the back-to-back work on the sequels. Moss has just finished filming on a serial-killer thriller, *Suspect Zero* which will be released in 2004.

Hugo Weaving

(Agent Smith): Hugo Weaving was born in Nigeria but spent most of his childhood in Bristol, where he lived long enough to take his O levels. He and his family moved to Australia in 1976. Weaving has been married to Katrina since 1984, and they have two children together – Harry and Holly.

Weaving's early acting career consisted mostly of bit-parts in Australian mini-series such as *Bodyline* (1984) and *The Dirtwater Dynasty* (1988). His first major role came in 1989, when he played Nicole Kidman's lawyer in the brutal prison drama *Bangkok Hilton* (Directed by Ken Cameron), in the story of an Australian woman imprisoned in a Thai prison for drug smuggling. Despite this high-profile role and then taking the lead in *Proof* (Jocelyn Moorehouse, 1991) opposite Russell Crowe, Weaving's career seemed to be restricted to fame inside Australia only.

However, Weaving's starring role as a confused drag queen alongside Guy Pearce and Terrence Stamp in *The Adventures Of Priscilla, Queen Of The Desert* (Stephan Elliot, 1994) brought him to an international audience. He lent his voice to Rex the Sheepdog in the family favourite *Babe* (Chris Noonan, 1995) and its sequel (George Miller, 1998) and appeared in gender-angst drama *Bedrooms And Hallways* (Rose Troche, 1998) before stepping into the sharp suit and shades of Agent Smith. *The Matrix* was just one of two trilogies that concluded in 2003 and featured Weaving in the castlist – the other being Peter Jackson's labour of love, *The Lord Of The Rings* (2001/2/3) in which Weaving played Elrond, Elvish leader. Weaving can next be seen in the family drama *Peaches* (Craig Monahan, 2003).

Gloria Foster

(The Oracle): Well-regarded stage actress Gloria Foster (born 15 November 1933) made her Broadway debut in the early 1960s as Ruth in Lorraine Hansbury's *Raisin in the Sun*. Her first film appearance came with the release of *Cool World* (Shirley Clarke, 1963), and her other film rolesoutside of *The Matrix* films include *Leonard Part 6* (Paul Weiland, 1987) and *City Of Hope* (John Sayles, 1991). Foster died on 29 September 2001 of a diabetes-related illness. She had completed most of her scenes for *The Matrix: Reloaded*, but none for *The Matrix: Revolutions*.

Joe Pantoliano

(Cypher): Joe Pantoliano (born 12 September 1951, New Jersey) has cornered the market in playing characters that could be fairly described as 'gits'. His films include *The Goonies* (Richard Donner, 1985), *Midnight Run* (Martin Brest, 1988), *The Fugitive* (Andrew Davis, 1993) and its sequel *U.S. Marshals* (Stuart Baird, 1998), and *Bad Boys* (Michael Bay, 1995). In 1996, he teamed up with the The Wachowski Brothers for *Bound*, in which he played mob-lord Caesar, frustrated by the double-dealing of his mafia colleagues and his gay-curious girlfriend Corky. On television he appeared in *L.A. Law* (1986), and played Ralph Cifaretto in two series of *The Sopranos*. Recently he had a supporting role in the Ben Affleck superhero flick *Daredevil* (Mark Steven Johnson, 2003), reprised his role of Captain Howard in *Bad Boys II* (Michael Bay, 2003), and has taken the lead in the forthcoming movie *Second Best* (Eric Weber, 2003).

| Supporting Cast |

Christine Anu

(Kali): Celebrated singer Christine Anu (born 1970) first came to worldwide attention when she sang the song 'My Island Home' at the Sydney Olympics Closing Ceremony. A popular leading lady on the Australian stage, she also played Arabia in *Moulin Rouge!* (Baz Luhrmann, 2001)

Julian Arahanga

(Apoc): Prior to playing Apoc in *The Matrix*, Kiwi actor Julian Arahanga appeared in the magnificent film *Once Were Warriors* (Lee Tamahori, 1994) and *Broken English* (Gregor Nicholas, 1996).

Helmut Bakaitis

(The Architect): Helmut Bakaitis (born 1944) is a much-respected stage director. He was the founding Artistic Director of the St Martins Youth Arts Centre in Melbourne, Australia, and former Artistic Director of the New Moon Theatre Co. He is currently serving as Head of Directing for the National Institute of Dramatic Art in Australia.

Monica Bellucci

(Persephone): Italian-born Monica Bellucci (born 30 September 1968) was one of the top fashion models in Milan before she made the leap to acting. One of her first major roles was as a bride of the eponymous count in

Bram Stoker's Dracula (Francis Ford Coppola, 1992). In this role, one of her major duties was to bestow vampiric kisses on Keanu Reeves – something she'd repeat in her role as Persephone. Other major films include *L'Appartement*, (Gilles Mimouni, 1996) – which co-starred her now-husband Vincent Cassel, *Under Suspicion* (Stephen Hopkins, 2000) and *Astérix & Obélix: Mission Cléopâtre* (Alain Chabat, 2002) in which she played the most famous pale-skinned Egyptian in history.

Recently, Bellucci played the lead role of Alex in Gaspar Noyé's controversial rape drama *Irréversible* (2002). Perhaps even more controversially, Bellucci has just completed work on Mel Gibson's next project, *The Passion*. Directed by Gibson in the original languages of the bible (Aramaic, Latin and Hebrew), it tells the story of the final days of Jesus Christ's life. Seemingly forever playing the temptress, Bellucci portrays Mary Magdalene.

Ian Bliss

(Bane): Having played Mr Bell in two series of *Heartbreak High*, Ian Bliss went on to star in the film *Bound* (Serhat Caradee, 2001) – not the Wachowski brothers' one, though that didn't stand in his way for playing the duplicitous Bane in the second and third *Matrix* films.

Daniel Bernhardt

(Agent Johnson): Daniel Bernhardt (born 31 August 1965) seems to be carving out a career for himself as an action hero, having previously starred in three of the *Bloodsport* sequels, taking over from legendary Jean-Claude Van Damme.

Marcus Chong

(Tank): Brother of Rae Dawn Chong, Marcus Chong (born 8 July 1967) was a regular castmember on the TV series *Street Justice* and the TV movie series *Vanishing Son* (John Nicolella, 1994). His first acting role was way back in 1974 when he appeared in the legendary twee TV nonsense *The Little House On The Prairie*. In 1995 he was one of the stars of *Panther*, Mario Van Peebles' film telling the story of the Black Panther movement. In 2003, Chong launched legal action against the Wachowski Brothers, claiming loss of earnings. This is because he claimed that the Wachowskis had promised him that his character Tank would return in the two Matrix sequel movies, whereas of course the character was killed off-screen prior to the beginning of *The Matrix: Reloaded*.

Collin Chou

(Seraph): Born on August 11 1967, Collin Chou has appeared in many Hong Kong action movies and is a former member of the Hung Ga Ban (Sammo Hung Stuntman Association). He's sometimes credited by his other acting names – Sing Ngai or Siu-Lung Chow. Chou was chosen to take over the role of Seraph in the two *Matrix* sequels after international chop-socky megastar Jet Li chose not to work on the films.

Steve Dodd

(Blind Man): Forget 'Follow the Rabbit', a fun game for *Matrix* fans watching other movies is 'Spot the Blind Man'. Steve Dodd has had small roles in a number of significant movies, including *Gallipoli* (Peter Weir, 1981), which starred a very young Mel Gibson, *A Cry In The Dark* (Fred Schepisi, 1988), which dramatised the famous 'Dingo murders' courtcase, *The Crossing* (George Ogilvie, 1990), which was one of Russell Crowe's first films, and *Quigley Down Under* (Simon Wincer, 1990), which saw Tom Selleck swap his Hawaiian shirts for outback cowboy gear.

Matt Doran

(Mouse): Matt Doran (born 30 March 1976) might be familiar to fans of Australian soap *Home and Away* where he played Damian Roberts (son of current regular character Irene Roberts) between 1992 and 1996. His film appearances include *The Thin Red Line* (Terrence Malick, 1998) and *Star Wars: Episode II – Attack Of The Clones* (George Lucas, 2002) in which he played Elan Sleazebaggano, a bar-room salesman who tries to sell Obi-Wan some 'death sticks'. He's also appeared in episodes of many TV series, including *Water Rats* (1997) and the imaginative sci-fi show *Farscape* (2001).

David Franklin

(Maitre D'): Franklin is yet another actor who has benefited from American TV shows being filmed Down Under, having bagged regular roles on fantasy series *Xena: Warrior Princess* (as Brutus) and *Farscape* (as Lieutenant Braca). His film appearances include two reptile-related features, *Crocodile Dundee In Los Angeles* (Simon Wincer, 2001) and *The Crocodile Hunter: Collision Course* (John Stainton, 2002).

Nona Gaye

(Zee): Nona Gaye (born 17 September 1974) is perhaps most famous because of her father – the legendary soul singer Marvin Gaye (famous for 'I Heard It Through The Grapevine', amongst many other classics). Following the terrorist attacks on the USA on September 11th 2001, Gaye (along with many other recording artists) released a cover version of her father's single 'What's Goin' On' in order to raise funds for charity. The role of Zee, Link's wife, was originally to have been played by R&B singer/actress Aaliyah, but her untimely death in a plane crash in 2001 meant that the role was recast, and Nona Gaye was successful in getting the part. Previously, Gaye had played Belinda Ali, second wife of the world's greatest boxer, in the biopic of Muhammad Ali (Michael Mann, 2001). Gaye's voice will soon be heard in the Robert Zemeckis-directed animation *The Polar Express* (due to be released in 2004).

Paul Goddard

(Agent Brown): Paul Goddard played Simon Armstrong in the Aussie soap *Sons and Daughters* from 1984/1985, and Stark in the science-fiction series *Farscape*. He has also appeared in a wide range of films, from the delightful *Babe* (Chris Noonan, 1994) to the ridiculous *Mighty Morphin' Power Rangers: The Movie* (Bryan Spicer, 1995), for which he should be thoroughly ashamed!

Deni Gordon

(Priestess): Deni Gordon played Ms Brooks in the Australian school drama *Heartbreak High* from 1995/1997.

Roy Jones Jr

(Ballard): Roy Jones Jr (born 16 January 1969) is not just an actor – he's also a professional boxer who, with his victory over WBA Champion John Ruizon on March 1 2003, became the first Light-Heavyweight since Michael Spinks to win a World Heavyweight Title. Appearing as himself, he guested on the hilariously vulgar comedy series *Married With Children* in 1996.

Randall Duk Kim

(The Keymaker): Randall Duk Kim's other films include *The Thin Red Line* (Terrence Malick, 1998) and *The Replacement Killers* (Antoine Fuqua, 1998). He also played General Alak in the non-musical version of *Anna And The King* (Andy Tennant, 1999) – a story more commonly known to most people as *The King and I*.

Harry Lawrence

(Old Man): In among 30 or so other TV and film roles, Harry Lawrence was one of the enthusiastic fans seen in *ABBA: The Movie* (Lasse Hallström, 1977).

Harry Lennix

(Commander Lock): Harry Lennix was a regular cast member of both *E.R.* and *Diagnosis Murder*, and his films include *The Five Heartbeats* (Robert Townsend, 1991), *Mo' Money* (Peter MacDonald, 1992), *Bob Roberts* (Tim Robbins, 1992), *Clockers* (Spike Lee, 1995) and *Get On The Bus* (Spike Lee, 1996).

Ada Nicodemou

(Dujour): Ada Nicodemou (born 14 May 1977) has been a regular cast member of Aussie soap *Home and Away* ever since she appeared in *The Matrix*; she plays Leah Poulos Patterson.

Harold Perrineau

(Link): Harold Perrineau starred in the first three series of the gritty HBO prison drama *Oz* as Prisoner #95H522 Augustus Hill. He also made a memorable Mercutio in *William Shakespeare's Romeo + Juliet* (Baz Lurmann, 1996).

Jada Pinkett Smith

(Niobe): One of Jada Pinkett Smith's first TV roles was as Lena in *A Different World*. She had small roles in *Menace II Society* (the Hughes brothers, 1993) and, as the pre-titles 'star' victim, in *Scream 2* (Wes Craven, 1997). Prior to *The Matrix* her most high-profile role was as the pretty Professor Purty in the Eddie Murphy remake of *The Nutty Professor* (Tom Shadyac, 1996). She starred opposite her real-life husband, Will Smith, in *Ali* (Michael Mann, 2001) as Muhammad Ali's first wife, Sonji.

Adrian & Neil Rayment

(The Twins): Without their shades and dreadlocks, real-life twins Adrian and Neil Rayment (born 14 May 1970) might be more familiar to British viewers as Carol Vorderman's assistants on the DIY show *Better Homes*. Talk about a change of pace – from rebuilding houses with Carol Vorderman, to blowing them away with Keanu Reeves...!

Tahei Simpson

(Binary): Tahei Simpson was a regular on New Zealand medical soap opera *Shortland Street* for the 1992 season.

Robert Taylor

(Agent Jones): Robert Taylor appeared in the ITV drama series *Yellowthread* Street and played Father Vincent Sheahan in the final series of BBC touchy-feely series *Ballykissangel.* He also appeared in the action-adventure film *Vertical Limit* (Martin Campbell, 2000).

Gina Torres

(Cas): On television, trained opera and jazz singer Gina Torres (born 1969) played Nebula, a recurring character on *Hercules: The Legendary Journeys*, Anna Espinosa on *Alias*, Zoë Warren on *Firefly*, and the awesome godlike Jasmine on the magnificent *Buffy the Vampire Slayer* spin-off show *Angel.* In 2002 she married Matrix co-star Laurence Fishburne.

Lambert Wilson

(Merovingian): Lambert Wilson is a prolific French actor (born 3 August 1958). His first movie role was opposite Jane Fonda and Vanessa Redgrave in Fred Zinneman's 1977 film Julia. Since then he's mostly appeared in French-language films, with more than sixty different pictures to his credit.

Where does the Matrix come from?

Back in 1999, one thing that most commentators discussing *The Matrix* agreed upon was that although the visuals were awesome and the action sequences groundbreaking, the plotline seemed somewhat familiar. It was as though every now and again you'd get a vague sense of déjà vu, of having seen key elements of the plot somewhere before. The Wachowski Brothers have themselves admitted that the first *Matrix* film contains many different references to mythology, history, literature and film. According to an online interview they took part in, the number of references are 'more than you'll ever know', so it's always fun to try to spot as many of these influences as possible. As the chapter on the names of the characters ('What's in a Name?') details the mythological and historical influences on the movies, here we'll examine the books, stories, comics, films and TV programmes that may well have had some impact on Larry and Andy's story telling. Of course, there's no way to tell if the brothers have indeed seen or read these sources, but the simple fact of their existence may well have impacted on the Wachowskis' creative process by proxy.

> In this chapter I'll talk in some depth about these sources and go into some detail about the plots and characters that seem to most closely match those in *The Matrix* films. I'll also include details on the books, movies, etc. so that you can either watch or read them yourselves and decide if *you* believe there's a connection!

Of course, there are entire genres of films such as Hong Kong Action films that had a major thematic influence on *The Matrix*, the movie that kick-started the use of wire-work in Hollywood movie stunt sequences. However, as many of these individual films are not particularly well known to Western audiences (or, in the case of *Crouching Tiger, Hidden Dragon*, were released into cinemas after *The Matrix*), you won't find them listed here. So, read on and discover just how some creaky old episodes of *Doctor Who* and the writings of Philip K. Dick may well have had some bearing on the genesis of *The Matrix*...

| Alice In Wonderland |

Directed by **Clyde Geronimi, Wilfred Jackson, Hamilton Luske** (1951)
Written by **Lewis Carroll** (*The Adventures of Alice in Wonderland*), writing team
Starring: **Kathryn Beaumont** (voice of Alice)

The explicit references to *Alice In Wonderland* throughout the first *Matrix* film are numerous – in fact, Neo's journey of discovery mirror's that of Alice in many ways. I've referenced the Walt Disney cartoon version of *Alice In Wonderland*, because the original two novels written by Lewis Carroll *(Alice's Adventures in Wonderland* and *Through the Looking Glass, and What Alice Found There*) are possibly less well known by the public, plus the plot of *The Matrix* tends to refer much more closely to the Disney adaptation. Thomas Anderson is told (while still in his 'real' world) to 'follow the white rabbit', just as Alice did before she fell down the rabbit hole and into Wonderland (in the books, Alice also falls into Looking Glass Land where everything is topsy-turvy). When Morpheus says to Neo 'I imagine right now you are feeling a bit like Alice... tumbling down the rabbit hole', we are forced to question what we're seeing on screen. Just as Alice couldn't work out what was real and what was fantasy, so Neo is beginning to question the reality of his own existence. Taking into account how the two original novels were written back in 1865 and 1871, the sophistication of Carroll's material is quite extraordinary, and just as relevant to audiences today as it ever was.

| Alien |

Directed by **Ridley Scott** (1979)
Written by **Dan O'Bannon, Ronald Shusett**
Starring: **Sigourney Weaver, Tom Skerritt, John Hurt, Ian Holm**

In 1979, director Ridley Scott created a brand-new look for science fiction, in which everything in the future was grimy, dirty and falling apart. Prior to this, anything 'futuristic' in films had always been bright, shiny and clean. By establishing a visual 'grunginess' to the characters' spaceship, the *Nostromo*, Scott single-handedly created the look and feel that practically every subsequent science-fiction movie has followed. How many SF films or TV shows have you seen since *Alien* feature gleaming shiny corridors or heroes dressed in tinfoil? No, everything is now dirty, from the clothes that look more like the type you'd see on a building site than in a NASA cockpit, through to the continually breaking down machinery. It's exactly this look and feel that matches the storyline and visuals of the *Matrix* films so well.

| Anime |

The Japanese animation industry has been thriving for the best part of ninety years, which is perhaps a little surprising to a Western audience that's only been aware of the genre for the past 15 years or so. The first ever Japanese animation was called *Mukuzo Imokawa the Doorman* (1917), which ran for the grand total of five minutes. For the early part of the twentieth century, anime tended to consist of a mix of Western-style animal cartoons and propaganda vehicles for the then military regime.

Following the Japanese defeat at the end of the Second World War, anime turned away from Western inspiration and began to take its ideas from Japanese comic books (known as Manga). For many years these anime adaptations of manga sources focused on fantasy plotlines, until in the early 1960s the legendary manga artist Osamu Tezuka adapted his own comic book *Astro Boy* into Japan's first ever full-length animated TV series.

From this point on, Japanese animation became much more prevalent, with series such as *Battle of the Planets* ('G-Force' in Japan) and *Ulysses 31* being major international successes. One of the most successful series in Japan was called *Gundam* (1981), which told the story of a huge war between Earth and its colonies in the distant future. By 1984, some animation studios were releasing direct-to-video feature films, largely consisting of either pornography or science-fiction titles. Unlike most other countries, the audience for animation in Japan consistently had a much older demographic, indeed, the animation studios actively targeted an older audience with much of their output.

The vast majority of the anime which crossed over to an international audience came from either direct-to-video or TV sources, that is, until the success of the cyberpunk thriller *Akira* in 1988. Written and directed by Katsuhiro Otomo, *Akira* is a cautionary tale of what goes wrong when a secret government project activates hidden supernatural powers and triggers a bloody coup against the government in Neo-Tokyo. Made on a much higher budget than most anime, *Akira* blazed a trail around the world and almost single-handedly made the Japanese animation industry one of the coolest on the planet.

Although *Akira* paved the way for anime, it is perhaps 1995's *Ghost In The Shell* that has the most direct impact on the

Matrix films. Directed by Mamoru Oshii, *Ghost In The Shell* is a futuristic thriller set in the not-too-distant future. The sinister government of this unnamed state utilises lifelike cyborgs for their undercover work. One such cyborg – the impossibly glamorous Major Kusangi – is sent on a mission to track down the super-hacker called The Puppet Master. Her journey of discovery leads her to question what it really is to be human. Can part-robotic beings truly think and feel in the same way that humans do? It's not just the thematic elements to the story of *Ghost In The Shell* that resonate with viewers of *The Matrix*, as there are many blatant on-screen sources that the Wachowski brothers may well have drawn upon. For instance, there are the full screens of bright green computer code; the concept of existing inside a gigantic computer-generated program; humans logging into the computer by literally plugging into a port embedded into the back of their necks; even the groovy agents of the government who wear high-fashion sunglasses whilst hunting rebels down with high-powered guns.

The Wachowskis have acknowledged the impact that anime had on the *Matrix* films. During an online interview (available at http://www.warnervideo.com/matrixevents/wachowski.html), they commented: 'We liked *Ghost In The Shell* and *The Ninja Scroll* and *Akira* in anime. One thing that they do that we tried to bring to our film was a juxtaposition of time and space in action beats.' Certainly it can be argued that *The*

Matrix was the first attempt at a live-action anime film, but it certainly wasn't the last (see **Deconstructing The Matrix** for more discussion on this subject).

| The Birds |

Directed by **Alfred Hitchcock** (1962)
Written by **Daphne du Maurier** (original story), **Evan Hunter**
Starring: **Tippi Hedren, Rod Taylor**

When the Sentinels begin their final assault on the *Nebuchadnezzar* in the final scenes of the first *Matrix* film, it's easy to think back to the climax of Alfred Hitchcock's classic thriller *The Birds*. Both feature an isolated environment, with a small bunch of heroes desperately fighting to save their own lives. Yet it's the way in which the non-human aggressors finally manage to gain access to the humans' refuge that seems the most familiar. A single breach is made in the defences, then a swarm of hostiles swoops through that hole. In certain shots, the angles chosen by the Wachowskis are nearly identical to those used by Hitchcock back in 1962.

| Conquest Of The Planet Of The Apes |

Directed by **J. Lee Thompson**
Written by **Paul Dehn**
Starring: **Roddy McDowell, Don Murray, Ricardo Montalban**

Yet another movie in the long-running *Planet Of The Apes* franchise, *Conquest Of The Planet Of The Apes* is unique in that it goes back in time to tell the story of how the Apes came to take over the running of the Earth. Just as the *Animatrix* story 'The Second Renaissance' details the way in which the machines stopped being mankind's servants and became its masters, this film shows the Ape revolution. Following a plague that has wiped out all other pets such as dogs and cats, monkeys are kept as household pets by most families but are treated more brutally than slaves. When one ape called Caesar (who's the son of talking apes from the future, but let's not get into that paradox right now!) decides that he's had enough of mankind's cruelty, he leads a revolt that brings about the subjugation of humanity. Do we hear any bells ringing?

| Dark City |

Directed by **Alex Proyas** (1998)
Written by **Alex Proyas, Lem Dobbs, David S Goyer**
Starring: **Rufus Sewell, William Hurt, Kiefer Sutherland, Richard O'Brien**

Rufus Sewell stars in *Dark City* as John, an ordinary man living in a bizarre, sinister city in this oddball movie that seemed to slip right underneath most cinema-goer's radar. John's life seems to be going from bad to worse: he's being hunted by the police for a series of murders he knows nothing about, a strange woman claims to be his woman and begins to hunt him down, as does a mysterious and sinister doctor. But weirdest of all are the Strangers, a group of powerful alien beings who seem to be pulling the strings of everyone who lives in the city. The Strangers are tracking down John, apparently because of the powers that he has started to manifest. John decides to get to the truth of the city – why does the daylight never arrive? And more importantly, why can nobody leave the city?

Thematically and visually, *Dark City* shares many elements with the *Matrix* films. Not simply a movie about a hero on the run from forces he cannot understand, it's also a tale of how people cope with powers they're not used to possessing. In particular, the design work of *Dark City* is an exercise in portraying a sinister future world while utilising elements of traditional 1940s Film Noir, something that *The Matrix* would refine the following year. Definitely worth watching, it's a shame that *Dark City* didn't make more of an impact at the box office: let's face it, any movie with Richard O'Brien in it can't be completely rotten...

| Philip K. Dick |

Science-fiction author Philip K. Dick was born in 1928 in Chicago, but lived most of his life in California. During his groundbreaking and revolutionary career, he wrote 36 novels and five short story collections, before his death in 1982. Most of Dick's writing covers themes such as hallucination, paranoia and schizophrenia alongside a technological setting, which makes it quite clear how his stories could have relevance to the creation of the *Matrix* films. Furthermore, although Dick wrote most of his important work in the 1950s through to the 1970s, he was amazingly prophetic about technology and how it would impact on the way society functions. In particular, Dick focused a lot of his storytelling on the power of the brain, the nature of reality, his distrust of government and how people deal with concepts like life, death and religion.

Dick's work reflects the rollercoaster of emotions he went through during his life, as his work was often inconsistent, veering from periods of intense creativity through to years of writers' block. He married on many occasions – none of them working out well – and spent much of his adult life addicted to drugs. Despite these problems, he managed to make a name for himself in the notoriously conservative 1950s by writing science-fiction stories that pushed the boundaries much further than those of other writers. His first published novel, *Solar Lottery*, was released in 1954, kick-starting a particularly creative and successful time in his career. However, it's the fiction of the 1970s that Dick is best known for today, from the Valis trilogy, through to the short story 'We Can Remember It For You Wholesale' and novel *Do Androids Dream of Electric Sheep* (filmed, respectively, as *Total Recall* and *Blade Runner*). Dick's writing has influenced a generation of Hollywood movie-makers and science-fiction writers and since his death at the age of 53, just prior to the premiere of *Blade Runner*, he has become widely regarded as a true visionary.

| Doctor Who: The Deadly Assassin |

Written by **Robert Holmes** (1976)
Directed by **David Maloney**

OK, so you're thinking, 'What on earth could the BBC's corny old science fiction series possibly have to do with *The Matrix*? Surely the only thing *Doctor Who* was about was motorised dustbins armed with sink plungers and egg whisks threatening the universe (provided there were no steps in the way)?'

Well, there's one *Doctor Who* adventure, first broadcast on the BBC in 1976, that features a staggering degree of similarity to the plotline of *The Matrix*. In 'The Deadly Assassin' (which raises the question of whether there any types of assassin which are not 'deadly'), the audience finally gets to see the home planet of the time-travelling Doctor. He returns to his home world of Gallifrey, where he is framed by his old enemy the Master for the assassination of the President of the Time Lords. In order to clear his name, the Doctor has to enter the Matrix.

Yes, that's right, I said 'enter the Matrix'. On Gallifrey, when a Time Lord gets old and dies, all of his or her memories are uploaded into a gigantic supercomputer called the

Matrix, the 'repository of all knowledge' in the universe. In order to clear his name, the Doctor enters the Matrix by lying down on a couch, where his brain is plugged into the giant computer. The Doctor's consciousness then reappears inside the virtual-reality world of the Matrix in an identical simulation of his body outside the computer. His enemy hunts him through a number of different locations, and even though the Doctor knows that the world around him isn't real – and indeed, is heard to cry 'I deny this reality!' – the stated fact is that should the villain win, the Doctor will die, in a very real sense, in the real world. In the end, the Doctor manages to overcome his opponent and eventually track down the real assassin.

Some ten years later, in a semi-sequel adventure called 'The Trial of a Time Lord', another virtual reality battle occurs inside the Matrix. This time, the Doctor's opponent is an evil version of himself, a being who appears to be able to assume the identity of other characters, literally becoming them in an attempt to confuse and defeat the Doctor.

However, these aren't the only occasions when *Doctor Who* touched on themes and plotlines that are found in *The Matrix* films. On several occasions the Doctor fought malign supercomputers intent on controlling an entire world full of humans. In 'The Face of Evil' (Pennant Roberts, 1977), the very next televised story after 'The Deadly Assassin', the Doctor has to defeat a computer called Xoanon. Xoanon has gone mad and instead of looking after and protecting the humans in its care, it decides to exert complete mental and physical control over the entire population. Much earlier, back in 1966, 'The War Machines' told the story of the first worldwide computer network, controlled by a single computer called WOTAN, which decided that humanity wasn't fit to govern itself and that machines would be much better in control. Finally, and earliest of all, during the first TV season of *Doctor Who*, way back in early 1964, a story called 'The Keys of Marinus' featured a society that had created a huge computer called the Conscience of Marinus, with the sole aim of controlling the emotions, thoughts and views of the population in order to prevent violence and subversion. Everything is fine until a warrior race call the Voord try to capture the Conscience in order to rule all of the humans on Marinus. Fairly prescient for a TV show most commonly dismissed for wobbly sets and dodgy special effects, eh?

| eXistenZ |

Directed and Written by **David Cronenberg** (1999)
Starring: **Jennifer Jason Leigh, Jude Law, Ian Holm, Willem Dafoe**

Arriving in cinemas scant months before *The Matrix*, *eXistenZ* is its spiritual twin, covering extremely similar ground but in an original and decidedly twisted fashion, much as you'd expect from director David Cronenberg, the twisted genius behind *Shivers*, *Rabid* and *Videodrome* (see below). Jennifer Jason Leigh stars as Allegra Geller, the world's leading game designer, who's testing the latest version of a new virtual-reality game she's created called eXistenZ. As she's about to test the game on a focus group, an assassin bursts in and tries to murder her with what appears to be an organically grown gun. Running for her life with a young man (played by a pre-megastar Jude Law), they are both forced to enter Allegra's virtual-reality game. Soon reality and fantasy merge into one confusing whole and nobody is really sure where the real world ends and a computer generated fantasy world begins. Sounds rather familiar, doesn't it?

Although it seems as though Cronenberg and the Wachowskis were covering similar ground, *eXistenZ* is actually a culmination of the themes that the Canadian horrormeister had been working on throughout his 25-year career; in particular body horror (items, normally mechanical, being inserted or removed from frail human flesh) and a questioning of what is reality and what is not.

| William Gibson |

Following on the creative inventiveness of Philip K. Dick, William Gibson adapted and updated the science-fiction genre in one fell swoop with 1984's novel *Neuromancer*. This one book created the genre of Cyberpunk, and won the Hugo, Nebula and Philip K. Dick awards in the same year. *Neuromancer* tells the story of Case, a computer cowboy able to cruise the information superhighway by plugging his consciousness into Cyberspace. After double-crossing the wrong people, Case's ability to rustle information is burned out of his brain, banishing him from Cyberspace. Eventually, a shadowy conspiracy offers Case a second chance, but at a price... Sounds very *Matrix*-y to me!

Not only did Gibson drag science fiction kicking and screaming into the 1980s and beyond, he also brought the 'science' element of science fiction to the forefront of current thinking. Gibson was one of the first writers to examine the impact of a huge interconnected network of computers on society, some ten years before the Internet became a household concept. Gibson, though, claims not to be a 'techie' himself: 'I don't know how these things work. But I like what they do, and the new human processes they generate' (see William Gibson's website www.william-gibson.com for more information). In many ways, the science-fiction concepts that Gibson described 20 years ago are now a fact of life. It remains to see what further concepts Gibson will create that may soon become familiar to us all.

| The Great Escape |

Directed by **John Sturges** (1963)
Written by **James Clavell, W.R. Burnett**
Starring: **Steve McQueen, James Garner, Richard Attenborough, Donald Pleasance**

The evergreen Bank Holiday Monday favourite, *The Great Escape*, is based on a true story and focuses on the largest Allied escape attempt from German prisoner-of-war camps during the Second World War. The only character that isn't based on a real individual is Steve McQueen's 'The Cooler Kid' and of course, it's his famous motorbike chase that undoubtedly inspired some of the fantastic motorway chase sequence in *The*

Matrix: Reloaded. Prior to *The Great Escape*, motorbikes hadn't seen much in the way of use in Hollywood chase sequences but after it they became the norm. McQueen was an accomplished biker and completed much of the sequence himself.

| Invasion Of The Body Snatchers |

Directed by **Don Siegel** (1956)
Written by **Daniel Mainwairing, Jack Finney, Sam Peckinpah**
Starring: **Kevin McCarthy, Dana Wynter, Larry Gates**

The ultimate in 'They're Coming To Get You' films, *Invasion Of The Body Snatchers* was inspired by an era in American history where paranoia was rampant. In the 1950s, Americans were convinced that Communist agents were at work within the USA, determined to infiltrate and undermine the ways of the free world. In the film, an alien race slowly begins to take over the bodies and minds of ordinary small-town Americans while they are asleep. When the town's doctor begins to suspect that something is wrong with the world, nobody believes him. The film was so successful that it was remade by director Philip

Kaufman in 1978 with Donald Sutherland. It's this updated version of the film that resonates in the original *Matrix* film. The scenes where Neo is fleeing towards his final escape from the Matrix, where ordinary members of the public turn on him and become yet more Agents, is scarily reminiscent of the sequences near the climax of the Body Snatchers remake where the alien versions of the population of San Francisco turn on the few surviving humans.

| The Invisibles |

Created by **Grant Morrison**

A groundbreaking and highly influential series of comic books, *The Invisibles* was first published in 1994 and ran for almost six years. *The Invisibles* is a tale of forthcoming Armageddon: on 22 December 2012, the world will come to an end, brought about by a race of inter-dimensional beings known as the Archons. Already the Archons are doing their best to ensure that the world will end on the day they expect it to, as throughout history they have worked in the shadows, manipulating kings and emperors and causing wars while ensuring that the general population knows nothing of their plans.

Fighting against the Archons and their agents of Control is a group of rebels and misfits called the Invisibles: an ancient and secret network of freedom fighters dedicated to the liberation and evolution of Humankind. Some of the Invisibles work alone, others contribute to the cause of freedom without ever knowing, simply by sabotaging 'the system' by refusing to go to school or by not buying into the latest mass-marketed product.

In *The Invisibles*, humanity has no idea that it is being controlled into subservience and obedience by an overwhelming force outside of its experience. It's left to King Mab's small group of anarchist terrorists to use whatever means it can to fight back against the Archons and let the rest of humanity know about the evil puppet-masters controlling them...

| Joe 90 |

TV Series, 1968
Created by **Gerry Anderson, Sylvia Anderson, etc.**
Starring the voices of **Len Jones, Sylvia Anderson, Rupert Davies**

After his enormous international success with the puppet series *Thunderbirds* and *Captain Scarlet*, Gerry Anderson's next 'Supermarionation' series was about a nine-year-old boy called Joe who becomes an agent for the World Intelligence Network. This is all thanks to a new technology that his father has developed to transfer specialist 'brain patterns' from any one person into his son's mind. As a result, Joe is able to become a test pilot, a brain surgeon and carry out many other impossible jobs and roles. Sounds remarkably like the uploading of skills into the brains of those connected to *The Matrix*, doesn't it?

| Johnny Mnemonic |

Directed by **Robert Longo** (1995)
Written by **William Gibson**
Starring: **Keanu Reeves, Dina Meyer, Ice-T, Dolph Lundgren**

Any movie starring Keanu Reeves in a futuristic nightmare where people are connected to a gigantic computer network has to be worth considering, but when it's been written by Cyberpunk legend William Gibson, the importance can't be underestimated. In *Johnny Mnemonic*, we're shown the world in 2021 where the entire planet is already connected to the Internet, and as a result, nearly half of the population is suffering from 'Nerve Attenuation Syndrome'. Johnny (Keanu Reeves) is a human courier who can carry huge amounts of data inside his own 'wet-wired' brain and his final mission is to transport the cure for NAS from Beijing to Newark. The problem? He's being hunted by two different organisations desperate to get their hands on the cure.

The major problem with *Johnny Mnemonic* is that the plot simply doesn't make much sense, primarily in the core concept: if the information is so valuable, then surely there has to be a safer way of transporting it than inside somebody's brain, especially when it's a last-gasp gambit. Lose Johnny, lose the information forever. In reality, despite the high-tech setting, this film is little more than a contemporary thriller, shrouded in an atmosphere of Cyberpunk-style.

| The Karate Kid |

Directed by **John G Avildsen** (1984)
Written by **Robert Mark Kamen**
Starring: **Ralph Macchio, Pat Morita, Elisabeth Shue**

For most Western kids in the 1980s, movies like Bruce Lee's *Enter The Dragon* were simply just too different from movies that they knew and loved to be culturally important. Sure, a few of the cool kids probably sat through some of his badly-dubbed chop-socky epics, but more were likely to have seen the rather dull parody in

The Kentucky Fried Movie (John Landis, 1977) and have absolutely no idea what Landis was taking the mickey out of. No, it was the huge mainstream success of *The Karate Kid* that really introduced the whole concept of martial arts to kids in the US and the UK, and what a success it was.

Ralph Macchio plays Daniel, a boy who moves to California from New York. Immediately he's the outsider amongst his schoolmates, and when he's beaten up by members of the local karate school he vows to fight back. Friendly local karate master Mr Miyagi (a marvellous portrayal by Pat Morita) helps Daniel to train in the 'secrets of the masters'. The scenes between Neo and Morpheus in *The Matrix* bear such a close relationship to the same scenes in *The Karate Kid* that it's hard to think that they didn't have some kind of bearing on the Wachowskis. However, I doubt if Morpheus would ever consider training Neo via the 'car wax on, car wax off' method.

| The Lawnmower Man |

Directed by **Brett Leonard** (1992)
Written by **Brett Leonard, Stephen King**
Starring: **Jeff Fahey, Pierce Brosnan, Jenny Wright**

Back in 1992, *The Lawnmower Man* was notable for two reasons; firstly for its cutting-edge computer generated graphics and

> secondly, for being the film that Stephen King successfully sued to remove his name from the credits. Coming a year after *Terminator 2: Judgment Day* revolutionised the use of CGI, *The Lawnmower Man* is sadly nowhere near as memorable and spectacular, but for a fan of *The Matrix*, its plotline would ring many bells. Jeff Fahey stars as Jobe, an educationally subnormal young man who becomes the target of the brain augmentation experiments of government scientist Pierce Brosnan. As with all top-secret government projects in the movies, the experiment goes horribly wrong. Although Jobe becomes able to absorb new skills in a remarkably short amount of time, he also develops both telepathic and telekinetic abilities, leading to a tragic showdown.

The cyberspace sequences of the film, in which Jobe learns his new skills, are quite basic by today's standards. However, the graphics themselves were all computer generated and showed movie-makers and the home games industry that high quality graphics were a reality and could provide a unique new set of tools for film-makers to use in the future.

| Logan's Run |

Directed by **Michael Anderson** (1976)
Written by **David Zelag Goodman, William F. Nolan, George Clayton Johnston**
Starring: **Michael York, Jenny Agutter, Farrah Fawcett Majors, Peter Ustinov**

Probably the most the most influential science-fiction movie of the 1970s prior to the arrival of *Star Wars* in 1977, *Logan's Run* became a huge international success and spawned a TV series that 're-imagined' the story. The movie is set in the year 2274, after a nuclear war has destroyed most of the Earth. The survivors of the holocaust now reside within a domed city, where everything at first appears happy and peaceful. However there is a terrible price to pay for this happiness: at the age of 30, all citizens take part in a ceremony called Carousel where they are 'renewed'. When policeman (Sandman) Logan discovers that 'renewal' is actually execution, he goes on the run with his friend Jessica to find Sanctuary, the place where people can be safe, happy and free from the control of the Sandmen. The similarities to *The Matrix* are very clear here, with an evil controlling government in the future, going on the run in the hope of finding a safe city in which to live, and being hunted down. It's still an extremely competent and highly entertaining film today.

| Minority Report |

Directed by **Steven Spielberg** (2002)
Written by **Philip K. Dick, Scott Frank, Jon Cohen**
Starring: **Tom Cruise, Colin Farrell, Samantha Morton**

Based upon a short story written by Cyberpunk maestro Philip K. Dick, *Minority Report* tells the story of a police officer in the not-too-far future working for a department that can arrest criminals before they are able to commit their crimes, thanks to the services of a group of 'pre-cognitive' seers who are plugged into a series of visualising machines. When the officer suddenly finds himself accused of a murder he has yet to commit, he is forced to go on the run from his own colleagues in an attempt both to prove that he will be innocent, and to find the real culprit before the crime can take place.

Of course, as this film was released after the release of the original *Matrix* film, the cinematic version can't have had an impact on the Wachowski brothers' magnum opus. It's the original Philip K. Dick short story that contains lots of elements which will be familiar to viewers of *The Matrix*:

a hero hunted down by an all-seeing state with people plugging into systems to give them different views of reality.

| 1984 |

Directed by **Michael Radford** (1984)
Written by **George Orwell** (novel), **Jonathan Gems, Michael Radford** (screenplay)
Starring: **John Hurt, Richard Burton**

George Orwell's legendary novel (filmed many times, most recently in the eponymous year itself) tells the story of a world after an atomic war. London has become the capital of the state of Oceania, a society ruled with an iron fist by a single political party. This party rules by fear, warning its citizens that 'Big Brother is Watching You', while observing every aspect of the lives of the citizens from on high. One lowly bureaucrat called Winston Smith does the unthinkable and disobeys Big Brother's orders by falling in love with Julia. Together they try to make their escape by avoiding Big Brother's listening and viewing devices. But of course, in Oceania, nobody can escape from Big Brother's gaze...

Winston and Julia's attempts to escape from Big Brother provide a lot of the thematic basis for Trinity and Neo's attempts to escape from the ever-present Agents of the Matrix. Furthermore, the horrific attempts by the Agents to torture Morpheus into revealing the truth about the rebels really do make the viewer think back to the similar torture sequences that Winston Smith undergoes in the terrifying Room 101. In an attempt to reinforce the thematic similarities between *1984* and *The Matrix*, have a look again at the first appearance of Neo in the first *Matrix* film. Specifically, have a look at the number of Thomas Anderson's apartment...

| The Quiet Man |

Directed by **John Ford** (1952)
Written by **Frank S. Nugent, Maurice Walsh**
Starring: **John Wayne, Maureen O'Hara, Victor McLaglen**

Featuring the ultimate example of a movie fist-fight, *The Quiet Man* stars legendary cowboy John Wayne as Sean Thornton, an American returning to his ancestral home town in Ireland to reclaim his birthright. Wayne's epic brawl with McLaglen's Squire Will Danaher lasts for so long that it makes the 'Burly Brawl' between Neo and the hundreds of Agent Smiths seem like it's over in seconds. Many movies have tried to equal the sheer energy of this punch-up, but until the *Matrix* films, very few have come anywhere near.

| Star Wars |

Written and Directed by **George Lucas** (1977)
Starring: **Mark Hamill, Harrison Ford, Carrie Fisher**

Surely you don't need to be told the plot of this one? It's the most influential film of the past 30 years, kickstarting the concept of a summer blockbuster film and making science fiction the most popular genre in cinema history. Nobody who was aged between five and 15 in 1977 and who's interested in films could possibly downplay the significance of *Star Wars* to them, and the Wachowskis are no different. And what is *Star Wars* all about? A young man accessing mystical energy to 'find' himself and thereby defeat the all-powerful bad guys. Yes, it's *The Matrix* all over again! Oh, and just to see how much the visuals of *Star Wars* impacted on *The Matrix*, have a look at the cockpit of the *Millennium Falcon* and the cockpit of the *Nebuchadnezzar*, and then decide if the two don't look mighty similar!

| Superman III |

Directed by **Richard Lester** (1983)
Written by **David & Leslie Newman**
Starring: **Christopher Reeve, Richard Pryor, Robert Vaughan, Annie Ross**

Superman III features one of the earliest instances in a Hollywood movie of a super-computer going beserk and trying to take over the world. The sequence in which the chief villainess (played by Annie Ross) is absorbed into the computer mainframe is particularly memorable and leads to the creation of a new machine villain that draws upon a human body to continue its campaign of destruction. There's also an extremely amusing scene where the villains create a virtual-reality shooting gallery in which they attempt to blow Superman out of the sky with their guided missiles hidden along the length of the Grand Canyon. Just as the *Animatrix* films 'The Second Renaissance, parts 1 & 2' detail how computers turn against the beings that created them, so *Superman III* shows what can go wrong when you don't have easy access to an 'off' switch that works. Thankfully the caped crusader shows up to prove to Richard Pryor the error of his ways. Phew!

| The Terminator / Terminator 2: Judgment Day |

Directed by **James Cameron** (1984/1991)
Written by **James Cameron, Gale Ann Hurd, William Wisher Jr**
Starring: **Arnold Schwarzenegger, Linda Hamilton, Michael Biehn, Edward Furlong**

Skynet, a super-computer built by humans, learns to think for itself, and in 1997 starts a nuclear war in an attempt to wipe out humanity. By the year 2029, the human resistance has almost been obliterated. Led by a man called John Connor, humanity decides to fight back. In *The Terminator*, the resistance sends a warrior back in time to the 1980s in attempt to save the life of a woman called Sarah Connor. She has been targeted for assassination by a time-travelling robotic killer, because she will give birth to the future leader of the resistance, John Connor. In *Terminator 2: Judgment Day*, Skynet sends an even more advanced killing machine back to 1995 in an attempt to kill both Sarah and her young son John.

Out of all of the films that have had a visual and thematic influence on *The Matrix*, it's perhaps *Terminator 2* that's the most overt. It was the first film to successfully utilise CGI in an action-movie environment, and in addition it gave viewers a brief insight into a futuristic earth decimated by machines. The blackened sky, the shattered landscape full of the wreckage of broken machines, the lethal machines tracking down the few survivors of humanity – all of these elements are clearly referenced in the *Animatrix* shorts (specifically 'The Final Flight Of The *Osiris*' and 'The Second Renaissance'). In fact, there are times that *The Matrix* seems as though it might even be an unofficial sequel to the *Terminator* films (although the release in Summer 2003 of a third *Terminator* film somewhat puts paid to that theory!).

| The Thirteenth Floor |

Directed by **Josef Rusnak** (1999)
Written by **Daniel F. Galouye, Josef Rusnak**
Starring: **Craig Bierko, Armin Mueller-Stahl, Dennis Haysbert, Gretchen Mol**

The *Animatrix* segment 'The Final Flight Of The *Osiris*' borrows some plot elements from this somewhat plodding thriller. When computer scientist Hannon Fuller uncovers a dangerous secret, he realises that his life may well be under threat. In order to ensure that this secret is safe, Fuller leaves a message for his colleague Douglas Hall inside the virtual-reality world that he's created. However, when Fuller is murdered, Hall becomes one of the prime suspects in the case. Hall is then forced to enter the virtual-reality re-creation of 1937 Los Angeles in order to track down the important clues that will clear his name. While the special effects are rather cool, the overall plot is somewhat flabby and some of the performances (sadly including the two leads Craig Bierko and Armin Mueller-Stahl) aren't really up to scratch, although it's nice to see an appearance from the future President Palmer of TV series *24*, actor Dennis Haysbert.

| THX 1138 |

Directed and Written by **George Lucas** (1971)
Starring: **Robert Duvall, Donald Pleasance**

Miles away from the simplistic 'cowboys and Indians in space' model of his most successful film, *Star Wars*, Lucas' THX 1138 is a much bleaker and more intelligent examination of a possible dystopian future that humanity could face. The movie tells the story of a society where people no longer have names of their own, just code numbers. Three individuals – THX 1138, LUH 3417, and SEN 5241 – attempt to escape from their subterranean society that has outlawed sex and utilised drugs to control the population. When THX

> 1138 stops taking the drugs, he gets LUH 3417 pregnant. For their crimes they are thrown in jail where they meet SEN 5241 and begin to plot how they can escape from the harsh rules of their society.

In THX 1138's world, it's technology and the system that's in control; individuals have no say about how they live their lives. All aspects of life are subservient to the ultimate goal of efficiency as they are monitored, manipulated and controlled by the soulless technology that runs the planet. It's odd for a science-fiction film that it gives no explanation as to how mankind ended up like this. Instead, viewers of this film are simply left with an unsettling portrayal of how humanity can become alienated if we become too reliant on machinery, systems and processes, a message that is all too clearly spelt out in the *Matrix* franchise.

| Total Recall |

Directed by **Paul Verhoeven** (1990)
Written by **Philip K. Dick** (story), **Dan O'Bannon, Ronald Shusett, Jon Povill, Gary Goldman** (screenplay)
Starring: **Arnold Schwarzenegger, Sharon Stone, Ronny Cox**

> Any film version of a Philip K. Dick story is undoubtedly worth revisiting if you're considering the influences upon *The Matrix* films. In *Total Recall* (based on Dick's story

'We Can Remember It For You Wholesale'), Arnie plays Douglas Quaid, a man haunted every night by the same dream about a journey to Mars. Trying to sort out his nightmares, Quaid visits Rekall Incorporated where he buys the memory of a holiday to Mars. However, this causes a massive brainstorm and soon Quaid can't remember if he's an ordinary earthbound construction worker or a secret agent fighting against the evil Mars administration.

Dealing in the loss of personal identity, fabricated memories and corrupt powerful organisations trying to prevent people from remembering the truth, there is much thematic goodness in *Total Recall* that's played out in more detail later in the *Matrix* films.

| Tron |

Directed by **Steven Lisberger** (1982)
Written by **Steven Lisberger, Bonnie MacBird**
Starring: **Jeff Bridges, Bruce Boxleitner, David Warner**

In 1982, Disney's computer fantasy *Tron* became a pioneering movie, showing audiences how the new worldwide fad of computer games could have a far more sinister side to it. In the film, programmer

> Kevin Flynn (Jeff Bridges) tries to prove that his former employers, ENCOM, have stolen his work. While investigating, he is accidentally digitised and absorbed into the ENCOM master computer. Flynn has to battle his way out of the computer's virtual world through a series of gladiatorial games, until eventually he teams up with a Security Program called Tron (Bruce Boxleitner). Together they join forces to defeat the power-mad central computer, the MCP (Main Computer Program).

Tron set new standards for animation, utilising early computers to generate stylised virtual landscapes into which the live-action performances of the cast were superimposed. Several sequences in *Tron* were so successful that they were, in turn (in a postmodern twist of epic proportions), made into sequences in the arcade game version of a feature film about arcade games! For a whole generation of film-makers, Tron was the first time in which the possibility of adventures taking place inside computers made an impression upon a willing audience.

| The Truman Show |

Directed by **Peter Weir** (1998)
Written by **Andrew Niccol**
Starring: **Jim Carrey, Ed Harris**

The box-office surprise hit of 1998 appears at first sight to have little in common with a high-tech science-fiction fantasy action movie. However, *The Truman Show* is all about one man's discovery that the world that he lives in is not actually what it appears to be. Truman Burbank's life has been entirely created by a disenchanted TV executive called Christof, whose goal of creating the 'greatest show on earth' has resulted in one man living a lie inside a reality designed and built specifically to house him. Although Neo shares his artificial reality with millions of other humans plugged into the Matrix, Truman is a lone dreamer. His fantasy is his alone, with the viewers at home fully aware of the scenario he lives in. Despite this, the journeys that both Truman and Neo go through are very similar – initial lack of knowledge, a dawning of the truth, followed by a determination to challenge the powers behind the false reality and break free of them.

| Videodrome |

Written and Directed by **David Cronenberg** (1983)
Starring: **James Woods, Sonja Smits, Deborah Harry**

A salutary warning of the dangers of losing the distinction between reality and what we see on TV, *Videodrome* is a horror film that mixes social commentary with some truly sickening images. James Woods stars as Max Renn, the controller of a small cable TV station who accidentally views a strange transmission that seems to show the torture and death of women. Trying to track down the source and discover if what he saw was a real snuff movie or just special effects, he discovers a terrifying plot to broadcast these images into the homes of millions of people – images that contain powerful subliminal messages to the audience. Slowly, Renn falls under the spell of the subliminal messages he has seen, losing his grip both psychologically and physically on the real world. Featuring some disturbing sequences, including a TV set that breathes and a stomach that opens up to accept a VHS video cassette and then plays it, it's the style and surreality of *Videodrome* that feels most like *The Matrix* films. But the most disturbing thing of all is the appearance by Blondie lead singer

Debbie Harry – you'll never be able to listen to 'The Tide is High' in the same way again...

| WarGames |

Directed by **John Badham** (1983)
Written by **Lawrence Lasker and Walter F. Parkes**
Starring: **Matthew Broderick, Dabney Coleman, Ally Sheedy**

Saturday Night Fever director John Badham tapped into yet another growing youth culture phenomenon in 1983 when he made *WarGames*, the tale of a young computer genius whose abilities cause mayhem. Matthew Broderick's character, David, finds a way to hack into the Pentagon's defence systems from the computer he has in his bedroom. David thinks that what he is hacking into is a space invaders-style training program – in reality, he breaks into the control systems for America's nuclear weapons. Can David get back into the system and tell the computer that World War III hasn't really broken out? Featuring more dark suited agents swooping on those lonely hackers than you can shake a stick at, *WarGames* is an essentially quite silly story that nevertheless caused quite a few sleepless nights for impressionable teenagers who thought that the end of the world could be a careless keystroke away.

| The Wizard Of Oz |

Directed by **Victor Fleming, King Vidor** (1939)
Written by **L. Frank Baum** (novel) and huge writing team (film)
Starring: **Judy Garland, Frank Morgan, Ray Bolger, Bert Lahr, Jack Haley**

Another children's fantasy novel that's probably more famous today because of the legendary film adaptation, *The Wizard Of Oz* is also directly referenced in *The Matrix*. Cypher tells Neo to 'buckle your seatbelt Dorothy, 'cause Kansas is going bye-bye', describing the scene from *The Wizard Of Oz* when young heroine Dorothy Gale is transported from her home in Kansas to the fantasy world of Oz thanks to a swirling journey through the eye of a tornado. Dorothy leaves the reality she knows and loves and ends up in a brightly coloured world populated by witches, munchkins and flying monkeys. One of the most famous 'tricks' of the movie adaptation is the switch from black-and-white photography to Technicolor. In the Kansas scenes at the start

> and end of the film, the real world is portrayed in monochrome, but when Dorothy journeys to Oz her 'fantasy world' shifts into beautiful bright colour. In *The Matrix*, Neo discovers that he's been living in a fantasy world all of his life. The original brightly hued colours of the 1999 Earth sequences dissolve into a reality of washed out, almost black-and-white images, in particular those of the shattered wreckage of the surface of the Earth. Furthermore, just as in *The Wizard Of Oz*, where the people in Dorothy's surroundings had counterparts in the dream world, so *The Matrix* characters have representations of themselves that look the same but have different abilities.

On a very basic level, Morpheus represents the mind and Trinity represents the heart of the group, just as the Scarecrow and the Tin Man were looking for those items in their own search through Oz. Cypher's cowardice paints him as the Cowardly Lion. In one way, Neo could be Dorothy going on a journey of discovery, the key to bringing everyone together in recognising their strengths. But given the fact that the crew of the *Nebuchadnezzar* is looking for him all along, it could be that Neo is in fact the Wizard of Oz himself. In Baum's story, the Wizard never realised his own ability either...

| The X-Files |

Created by **Chris Carter** (1993/2002)
Starring: **David Duchovny, Gillian Anderson, Mitch Pileggi**

Just as *Star Trek* had swept the globe in the 1960s, so *The X-Files* became the international science-fiction TV show hit of the 1990s. Although there weren't many episodes of the series that dealt with *Matrix*-style themes or plots (one notable exception being an episode written by Cyberpunk maestro William Gibson), it's the overall look and style of the series that's the most relevant parallel. For many years, science fiction had become a more 'tongue-in-cheek' style of genre, with the general public viewing it mostly as 'silly' or 'unrealistic'. When *The X-Files* arrived, suddenly there was a series that took its bizarre and surreal subject matter and dealt with it in a highly 'realistic' fashion, akin at times to a documentary or a 'proper' drama series. With an emphasis on lots of blue lighting, close camera angles and a cast that delivered every spurious line of dialogue with the utmost sincerity, *The X-Files* became the blueprint for the success of *The Matrix*.

DECONSTRUCTING THE MATRIX

Why exactly is *The Matrix* cool? Is the film a clarion-call to disenfranchised rebels everywhere, or merely a cynical attempt to extort yet more money out of a gullible population? Coming up is my take on the impact that *The Matrix* films have had on popular culture, and why it's been such a massive success for the corporate suits behind it.

| Geek legends |

Being able to identify with heroes in fiction is a very powerful concept. Right from the early months when your parents read you bedtime stories, it's vital that one of the leading characters is someone that the audience can identify with. For example, when reading the *Famous Five* stories by Enid Blyton, I'd wager that very few children read through them without being able to say which one of the Five was their favourite (put your hand down if you were going to say Timmy the dog!). Ensuring that the characters say something to their audience means that they become more emotionally involved in the content and are more likely to want to invest more of their time in that product and any related material.

This is precisely why the makers of *The Matrix* hit on a goldmine when they created their hero Neo. Knowing full well that most fans of science fiction have a reputation for being a bit geeky, the Wachowski brothers chose to make the hero of their film somebody with perfect nerd qualifications: a computer programmer who has very little life of his own, no friends and a dead-end job. Thomas Anderson even appears to have poor communication skills, never really being seen getting into a proper conversation with anyone. Could this even potentially be a mild case of Asperger's Syndrome, a mild form of autism that manifests itself in people who are unable to judge the standard social norms during a conversation? For instance, they don't hold eye contact or pick up on signals when people start getting bored with their conversation, so it could be argued that Thomas Anderson's own characteristics reflect these symptoms early on in the movie.

Thankfully, in *The Matrix* there is hope for anorak-wearing geeks everywhere! When Thomas Anderson becomes Neo, there's a massive shift in what he looks like and how he behaves. Now he's not socially inadequate, hanging around unable to speak to people in nightclubs. Instead he's the coolest of the cool, a slick customer who's a leader of men, a daring hero able to sweep the gorgeous Trinity off her feet and into bed. In short, Neo becomes even more of an aspirational hero figure for the primary audience watching *The Matrix* films. Plug yourself into *The Matrix* and you too can become cool! Buy the sunglasses, the mobile phones. Listen to the soundtrack album, and buy a long black trenchcoat. In short, what *The Matrix* films tell their audience is that it is possible to leave innate geekdom behind. All you have to do is buy the right products and social acceptance will finally be yours. Gone are the days when wearing black all the time marked you out as being a freak because black is, well, the new black.

But hang on a second. Doesn't this go entirely against the message of freedom, independence and non-conformity that the movies extol? When Morpheus assembles his army of unplugged warriors to fight back against the evil brainwashing machines, the one thing that he promises is freedom from control.

Unplug from the Matrix, and you will finally be able to decide what you want to do, to take control of your own destiny. In short, you'll be able to be an individual ('Yes, we are all individuals', as a group of followers once said to their Messiah). However, this message of freedom and individuality seems to conflict with the marketing messages that *The Matrix* franchise bombards us with.

| Buy, buy, buy! |

In the film *Fight Club* (David Fincher, 1999), Tyler Durden (Brad Pitt) teaches his followers that the only way to be free in modern society is to stop being defined by the objects that you own. You are not defined by your job, your clothes or your Ikea coffee table, he declares. That's certainly not an attitude that the marketing men who work for major film studios would approve of. Many months before the eventual release of a feature film, it's common practice to start promoting the movie through tie-in marketing campaigns. For *The Matrix* films, these campaigns have tended to revolve around certain of the featured 'toys': mobile phones, TVs, sunglasses, etc. The first places that advertisements for these products tend to appear are the high-end 'lifestyle' magazines such as *Vanity Fair*. These aren't specifically aimed at the consumers who will eventually buy these products, but are pitched directly at the style leaders and trend-setters who will then go on to write features for their own magazines on what's 'cool', what's 'in' and just exactly what all of the most painfully fashionable people on the planet simply have to own, darling.

In the weeks immediately prior to the release of a film, you'll often begin to see large billboard poster campaigns, magazine features and even TV adverts, all of them selling a specific product, but usually by showing its careful placement within the film. For example, prior to the release of *The Matrix: Reloaded*, Samsung ran a multi-media marketing campaign for its mobile phones and TV/monitors, carefully utilising either clips or still photographs from the forthcoming movie to reinforce their own brand. Furthermore, associating extremely cool and desirable brands with the name 'Matrix' helps to convince an information-hungry audience that taking the time and effort to go and see the film is going to make them trendy and socially acceptable. It's a perfect case of 'you scratch my back and I'll scratch yours' that results in both brands seeing their profits and profile rise enormously. We haven't even begun to mention the premium that corporations pay to the movie industries for the privilege of having their particular product 'placed' into a hit film.

What these messages sell to their target audience is the concept of the modern world as a new playground for adults to indulge their fantasies in (note the use of the empty school playground, the venue for the 'burly brawl' between Neo and the dozens of Agent Smiths, in the advertising for mobile phones). As we grow up, we no longer 'put away childish things', we just replace the toys we played with as children with new versions specifically designed to appeal to adults. It's not without good reason that acquiring the latest mobile phone with the up-to-the-minute features or making sure that you're driving the trendiest car is often described as a 'boys' toys' fixation. Thankfully for the money men of these big corporations, grown-ups tend to have a great deal more disposable income to spend than just 50p pocket money.

As I mentioned earlier, this message to 'buy, buy, buy' seems in direct conflict with the anti-authoritarian attitude portrayed by our heroes in *The Matrix* films. In fact, their message is to say 'no' to consumerism, to be yourself, to be not taken in by the messages being pumped into your mind. Naturally, nobody is seriously going to stop being a consumer of mass-marketed products just because they've watched a film that tells them to say no to consumerism. In fact, seeing such a message in a film is more likely to cause precisely the opposite effect. I'm sure that many people came out of the cinema having watched the first *Matrix* movie thinking 'yeah,

> the world is mad! I'm not going to be brainwashed any more!' The same people, having been inspired to question the way in which they look at the society in which they live, will almost certainly have been the same people that rushed to buy a copy of *The Matrix* on DVD as soon as it was released. And where did the money they spent on that DVD go to? A small proportion to the Wachowski Brothers, perhaps, but the bulk of it to went to the major retail chain they bought the DVD from, and of course to the movie studio that made the film in the first place. Very liberating! And of course, wanting to buy into the mindset of *The Matrix*, you've just bought a book on the subject, haven't you?

In fact, the biggest fans of *The Matrix*, the ones who really wanted to find out more about the film and how it was made, probably bought more than one copy of the film on DVD. In fact the film has been released in two different 'editions'. The second release is a double disk set, in which you get a supplementary disk full of documentaries and information that go into painstaking detail about why *The Matrix* is such a quality product. By buying the disk and watching it, you find yourself drawn still further into your commitment to the brand, spending more of your time finding out still more about the same product. This cross-referencing and cross-marketing has been very carefully exploited by the Wachowskis in the products they have created to support the release of the two sequel movies. It's not essential to have watched *The Animatrix* DVD to understand the plot of *The Matrix: Reloaded*, but of course it helps. When the overly enthusiastic kid runs up to greet Neo and Trinity, the real fans will already know that it's the same kid who makes his escape from *The Matrix* in the *Animatrix* short 'Kid's Story'. Similarly, the much-hyped presence of Jada Pinkett Smith in the sequel seems to be little more than a glorified cameo – but the players of the *Enter The Matrix* computer game will have found out a lot more about who she is and her involvement in the grand scheme of things. If you're a real fan, you'll buy still further into the brand, finding yourself wishing to remain plugged into the constructed reality being peddled to you by the controlling forces of the corporations. Who said that the money men didn't have a sense of irony?

| Insecure, moi? |

In the Oscar-winning documentary *Bowling For Columbine* (Michael Moore, 2002), the question of why American society is so obsessed with guns is examined. Michael Moore describes a society that can be quite scary to those of us brought up in the UK, where gun crime is thankfully still relatively rare and every death by shooting still makes the evening news. Moore comes to the conclusion that the dominant factor in the American plague of gun-related deaths is down to fear, not just the proliferation and availability of handguns.This is an interesting concept that's well worth applying to the world of *The Matrix*.

> Firstly, have a think for one moment about the spam emails that you receive in your inbox every morning. Quite apart from being the single most irritating phenomenon in the world right now, it's very telling to have a look at what those emails consist of. In short, they all play on your deepest, darkest fears. Get out of debt! Get a bigger penis! Lose weight now! Become more attractive to girls! Your computer is at risk from people snooping on you! By implanting these fears directly in your inbox, the email spammers are invoking one of the oldest tricks in the book: using your fear to provoke a response and thereby part you from your cash. One of the most prolific TV advertising campaigns in the UK uses precisely this theory to promote its services. 'Ashamed of your mobile?' the adverts ask, encouraging you to worry (for the first time, if you have any sense whatsoever) that you may become less hip and trendy, lose friends or even become a social pariah if you don't own the 'right' mobile phone.

In *The Matrix*, we see how this method is used to extremely good effect. In Thomas Anderson's world he's bawled out by his boss, who uses fear to generate a response of obedience. By threatening to take away Thomas's job, his boss maintains the status quo of control: Thomas doesn't have it, and he can't do anything about it. Thomas is even ridiculed because he apparently believes that he's 'something special', with his boss attempting to retain control by reminding him that the rules that everyone else adheres to apply to him as well. This plays on everyone's core employment fears, such as 'Does my job define me as an individual? Does it represent who I would like to be seen as to strangers and friends alike? Does my boss see me as an individual, or just as a statistic?' It's only when Thomas chooses to assert his individuality and completely reject everything to do with the system that's controlling him that he's able to find his freedom. In a world where the type of fear you have defines you as a person, the ability to shake off fears that are imposed on you by external influences is the quickest path to true freedom.

| Anarchy in the USA |

By rebelling against the control of *The Matrix* and freeing himself, Neo addresses a question that has plagued people ever since mankind first began to huddle together in communities: If I get rid of the people in control, who will take their place? More importantly, can any government be better than another? When the humans were plugged into the virtual-reality simulation created by the Matrix, they believed at the time that they were free. The concept of what freedom actually is is an important one that is addressed on many occasions in the *Matrix* films, and it's one that's equally applicable to the world in general right now. Americans have a proud claim that their country is 'the land of the free', but what does that actually mean? Some Americans argue that the reason for their freedom is their Constitution, a document that enshrines the right of each individual to liberty, to the right to carry firearms, to a whole host of different privileges.

> Well, actually, no. The Constitution by its very nature is a list of rules and responsibilities, a set of boundaries that American society has agreed to abide by in order to preserve law and order. By its very definition the Constitution represents the complete opposite of 'freedom': adherence to a rigidly defined set of rules and regulations. While he was still inside the Matrix-generated world of 1999, Thomas Anderson obeyed the rules and regulations established by the system. Although we know that this Thomas was actually not 'free' as such, let's look at how his life ran. He worked in his job, and provided he got into work on time, he could rest assured that his boss was unlikely to try to murder him at the earliest possible opportunity. He was able to hang out in his own apartment whenever he wanted, associate with some dodgy friends and spend much of his time surfing the Internet. Sounds like about 90 per cent of the 14–35 age range in the UK, I reckon…

Compare this life of 'captivity' with the freedom that Neo was able to enjoy following his unplugging from the Matrix. Neo and his friends are consistently persecuted and hunted down by an army of unstoppable Sentinels determined to kill them at the earliest opportunity. His body is perforated with dozens of gaping holes (surely a major problem with getting infections or at the very least breadcrumbs trapped in them!), he follows the instructions given to him by his new leader Morpheus and he even has a quarter of a million people worshipping him as their saviour. On top of all of those problems, Neo even discovers that his entire life outside the Matrix has been pre-ordained and as such he has little or no control whatsoever over how that life will unfold. What kind of freedom is this? Perhaps Cypher had the right idea.

> The reality of the life facing Neo in the 'real' world is one where he has just replaced one set of controls with another. As viewers we are strongly led to believe that being 'plugged in' is wrong, but who are we to pass that judgement? If the audience is being asked to make a moral judgement between two different sets of controls, then surely the whole debate about freedom is a bit of a sham. Hippies would undoubtedly argue that the only true freedom is to exist in a world without any kind of rules or regulations, and that's what Neo promises to deliver in his rousing speech at the end of *The Matrix*. But is humanity ready to accept a total absence of rules, or as it's otherwise known, anarchy? Could that be what Neo will eventually bring to the humans still plugged into the Matrix – a path to the first genuine 'land of the free', a land of anarchy?

| The bourgeoise and the rebel |

Take a glance at the track listing on *The Matrix* soundtrack album (as a fan of *The Matrix*, you do own the album, don't you? Of course you do!) and you'll notice that practically every track conforms to one single genre, colloquially known by 'the kids' these days as 'Nu Metal'. Why did the Wachowski Brothers choose to use this style of music? Well apart from fitting with the frenetic pace of the movie itself, it taps into the key demographic group at which their movie is targeted: disenfranchised youths who feel that they don't belong, who think that there must be something wrong with the way in which the world is operating. This is an example of darned clever marketing. By providing a selection of tracks by artists that closely match that demographic, the record company can more or less guarantee that they will shift significant quantities of the soundtrack album, generating a healthy profit through a minimum amount of effort.

| WARNING! Deconstruction work ahead |

I'd like to ask you to do a little experiment for me. The next time you have access to a computer, go to one of the major search engines, enter the word 'Matrix' and hit return. How many different results does it come up with? Well, I did just that in early July 2003, and got 14.4 million results. Yes, over 14 *million* websites that could be of interest to Matrix fans.

That's an impressive figure, don't you think? What this means is that there are over 14 million other websites that you could visit that have nothing whatsoever to do with the official *Matrix* site, www.whatisthematrix.com. All around the globe, people who really love the *Matrix* films have decided to let their fingers do the talking and create their own sites. The huge proliferation in fan websites is a major phenomenon in itself, but let's face it, many of those sites would undoubtedly disappear as quickly as they arrived if there wasn't an audience to read the content created by them.

Having access to unofficial information about something you like is one of the great benefits of the Internet age. Before the advent of the home surfer, such a concept would have been almost unthinkable. Organisations were used to being able to control all the information in circulation about their product, and any attempt to undermine the corporation's copyright was stamped on rapidly. Thanks to the Internet, people are able to take a kind of virtual 'ownership' over the brands and products in which they have invested their time and emotions. As a result of this 'ownership', some online communities of fans have developed to such an extent that they actually begin to demand more and more from the creators of the product they are fond of and even begin to get angry when

> their requests for information fall on deaf ears. The Internet is truly beginning to rewrite the rules of how we enjoy the entertainment that's provided to us, and the wise corporation does what it can to meet the needs of the loyal online community.

Unofficial websites have a kind of glamour and thrill to them that the official sites will never have, no matter how much unique downloadable content, official interviews or whatever may be available there. An extra benefit to the studios of unofficial websites is the viral marketing potential they bring. If people are talking online with their friends in communities or creating websites extolling the virtues of their upcoming product, then that gives a much-needed extra boost of credibility. We're all very used to taking the quotes we see on a movie poster with a pinch of salt, but when we see a member of the public dedicating their own time and effort into 'bigging up' the same film, we're much more inclined to take it seriously. Viral marketing like this is becoming a technique that the major movie studios are using themselves. Ever since the hype surrounding *The Blair Witch Project* (Daniel Myrick and Eduardo Sanchez, 1999), a film that relied solely on Internet word-of-mouth to generate bums-on-seats, this phenomenon became more appreciated. Rumour has it that certain movie companies have begun to create their own 'fan sites' for their forthcoming projects, in the hope that viral marketing will help boost the box office take on the opening weekend.

Rather than cracking down on unofficial and unauthorised websites, it's in the best interests of the movie corporations to allow such activity to flourish. In a similar way, the actions of the rebels inside *The Matrix* only serve to strengthen its grip on those under its control. As we discover at the end of *The Matrix: Reloaded*, the entire program has been constructed on the premise that there will always be rebels that will try to shut it down. It anticipates this behaviour and is able to destroy any major threat with a minimum of effort. As long as fans online don't do anything to threaten the success of their project, there's no reason to worry too much about any lethal legal attacks from the people in control...

100
100
100
001
000
101
010
100
110
100
001
100
100
101
000
010
100
001
011
000
010
110
101
000
101
011
101
001
001
010
101
010
101
001
001
011
001
001
000
010
001
010
101
001
101
000

APPENDICES

100
100
100
001
000
101
010
100
110
100
001
100
100
101
000
010
100
001
011
000
010
110
101
000
101
011
101
001
001
010
101
010
101
001
001
011
001
001
000
010
001
010
101
001
101
000

THE ANIMATRIX

Just two weeks after the UK release of *The Matrix: Reloaded*, Village Roadshow Films and Warner Home Video released on DVD and VHS a collection of nine short animated films called *The Animatrix*. These nine shorts (or more accurately eight, as 'The Second Renaissance' was split into two separate halves for some odd reason) offer *Matrix* buffs a valuable series of new ideas and concepts that help to fill in a great deal of the 'backstory' behind the cinematic films. In addition, they also give viewers a deeper insight into aspects of *The Matrix* that they may not have previously considered.

Some of the *Animatrix* shorts are, quite simply, works of genius, others are perhaps less striking. All of them, however, feature some of the most ground-breaking computer-generated animation yet seen in the cinema, with 'The Final Flight Of The *Osiris*' and 'A Detective Story' being worthy of particular praise.

A detailed breakdown of *The Animatrix* package is included here as an appendix, as it's very much a separate project from the rest of the *Matrix* saga.

Warner Bros. Presents
In association with Village Roadshow Pictures
and NPV Entertainment
The Animatrix

Produced by **Larry and Andy Wachowski**

Executive Producer	**Joel Silver**
Co-Producer	**Steve Richards**
Associate Producer	**Phil Oosterhouse**
Segment Producers	**Michael Arias, Hiroaki Takeuchi, Eiko Tanaka**

Music Composed by **Don Davis**

Casting and Voice Direction	**Jack Fletcher**

Animation Produced by **Marvelous Entertainment Inc and Softimage Co**
Production Support Services by **Comix Wave Inc**

Script/Story Consultant	**Anthony Weintraub**
Producer	**Hiroaki Takeuchi**
Production Co-ordinator	**Nozomi Seike**

Production Assistant **Kazuki Sunami**
Chief Technical Officer **Mitsuhiro Amano**
Additional Score by **Chris Neilman, Mark Kilian and Adam Schiff**

| The Final Flight Of The *Osiris* |

Written by **Andy and Larry Wachowski**
Directed by **Andy Jones**
Computer Animation, Design and Production by **Square USA, Inc.**
Supervising Editor **Zach Staenberg**
Co-Producer **Spencer Lamm**
Thadeus **Kevin Michael Richardson**
Jue **Pamela Adlon**
Crew Man **John DiMaggio**
Operator **Tom Kenny**
Pilot **Rick Gomez**
Crew Woman **Tara Strong**
Old Woman **Bette Ford**
Computer Animation Design and Production, Produced by **Jun Aida**
Computer Animation Design and Production, Executive Produced by **Cameron Stevning, Jary Mundell and Junichi O. Yahagihara**
Production Designer **Owen Paterson**
Costumes Designed by **Kym Barrett**
Lead Animator **Matthew T. Hackett**

'Conga Fury'
Written by Mabi Thobejane and Ben Watkins
Performed by Juno Reactor
Courtesy of Waxtrax! Records/TVT Records

Storyline:

Inside a Dojo fighting arena, two athletic and nubile swordspeople are undergoing a rigorous workout – but astonishingly they are doing it blindfold! Attack after attack seems to pass millimetres away from their flesh, occasionally slicing away bits of clothing. The two warriors – Thadeus and Jue – are about to share a kiss in the middle of their battle when a warning klaxon sounds... and the couple reappears in the real world. They are on board a ship called the *Osiris* (Mark VI, No.16 – Made in the USA, Year 2079) and it seems that there are Sentinel machines nearby.

In fact, the rest of the crew of the *Osiris* seems shocked by what the sensors are telling them, because there are literally thousands of Sentinels directly above them. Spotting some more Sentinels nearby, Captain Thadeus orders that the *Osiris* should take an uncharted intersection in a desperate escape bid. A small group of Sentinels locks on to the *Osiris* and moves in for the kill, but the crew returns fire with a blistering series of blasts from the ship's weapons.

To Thadeus's surprise, the uncharted pipeline takes the *Osiris* above ground and into the 'real' world, the remains of what was left of humanity's original cities after the machines took over.

From the bridge of the *Osiris*, the crew can see what appears to be a vast drilling machine with thousands of Sentinels swarming all around it. Thadeus suddenly realises that Zion, the last free city of mankind, lies four kilometres directly beneath the drilling point. It's clear that the machines have decided to attempt an alternative method of destroying Zion, and that boring directly down from the surface of the Earth to the underground city is the quickest way of achieving their aims.

At that moment, the Sentinels notice the proximity of the *Osiris* and thousands upon thousands of the deadly machines begin pouring towards the human ship. The *Osiris* beats a hasty retreat, all guns blazing. However, Thadeus realises that they are completely outnumbered and that the ship is almost certainly doomed. Thadeus decides that the information about the terrifying drilling equipment needs to be passed on to the people in Zion, but he also realises that there is no way that the *Osiris* and its crew will be able to physically get back to the city before they are destroyed. Instead, Thadeus proposes a plan to Jue: she will go into the Matrix and leave a parcel of information at a specific information drop point in the hope that one of the rebels finds it before the Agents and programs inside the Matrix destroy it. Realising that their time together is over, Jue eagerly volunteers.

As Sentinels begin to swarm all over the *Osiris*, Thadeus and Jue share a final kiss before he connects her back into the Matrix. As the probe is inserted into the back of Jue's head, she mentally reappears inside the Matrix's 'real' world of 1999 Earth. In a desperate race against time, she leaps and somersaults from building to building, heading for the drop point where she will leave the vital information. As the *Osiris*'s hull is breached, the crew is picked off one by one by the lethal Sentinels through a combination of deadly lasers and even more unpleasant spiked and bladed tentacles. No longer being piloted, the *Osiris* crashes down on to the surface of the scorched and desolate Earth before being swamped by still more Sentinels.

Jue finally reaches the information drop point and places a recording of the *Osiris*'s discovery into a letter box. Mere seconds after Jue deposits her vital cargo, the *Osiris* explodes, killing everyone on board. Inside the Matrix, the lifeless body of Jue collapses to the floor.

Commentary: 'The Final Flight Of The Osiris' is a fantastic piece of filmmaking, full stop. Quite apart from the cutting-edge CGI used to animate this story, it's a riveting tale of sacrifice, determination and really great-looking people losing parts of their clothing bit by bit. In story terms, it's a direct prologue to *The Matrix: Reloaded*, telling of the discovery by humanity of the machines' final attack on Zion. Keeping you right on the edge of your seat until the final sad (yet curiously uplifting) conclusion, this is one of the highlights of the *Animatrix* project.

| The Second Renaissance (parts 1 and 2) |

Story by **Larry and Andy Wachowski**
Written and Directed by **Mahiro Maeda**
Animation and Production Design by **Studio 4°C**, Tokyo

The Instructor (Zion Archive)	**Julia Fletcher**
01 Versatran Spokesman	**Dane Davis**
Kid	**Debi Derryberry**
Mother	**Jill Talley**
Additional Voices	**Dwight Schultz, James Arnold Taylor, Jill Talley**
Animation Producer	**Eiko Tanaka**
Production Design	**Hideki Futamura**
Art Director	**Atsushi Morikawa**

'Big Wednesday'
Written by Adam Freedman, Jamie Stevens and Frank Xavier
Performed by Free*Land
Courtesy of Marine Parade

'Ren2'
Written and Performed by Photek

'Dark Moody'
Written and Performed by Junkie XL
Courtesy of Roadrunner Records

'Supermoves'
Written by Robert Howes
Performed by Overseer
Courtesy of Columbia Records
By arrangement with Sony Studio Licensing

'Martenot Waves'
Written by John Steven Corrigan
Performed by Meat Beat Manifesto
Courtesy of North Star Media

Storyline: 'Welcome to the Zion Archive. You have selected Historical File Number 12/1. The Second Renaissance.' A softly spoken computerised female voice begins to tell the story of the Second Renaissance, the rebirth of a new era of enlightenment. 'In the beginning, there was Man. And for a time, it was good…' The Zion archive file shows scenes from twenty-first-century Earth, a time of plenty and of decadence for the human population and a time for menial tasks for the robots and other machines that mankind had constructed. As the years went by, humanity created machines that were increasingly complex; machines that began to think and reason for themselves. Despite this, the machines continued to work tirelessly to do man's bidding, creating new buildings, cities and empires.

Although the machines were loyal to their masters, they had no respect. They were, after all, just machines. Then one day, a robot called B166ER rose up against his human masters and ripped them to pieces. At B166ER's trial,

> the prosecution argued for the owner's right to destroy his own property. In his defence, the robot argued that he simply did not want to die. Many voices were raised in B166ER's defence – if the machine had been built in man's own image, who was to say that the machine did not have exactly the same 'spark of humanity' that man possesses? However, realising the massive instability that would come about from granting freedom – the vote – the right to life – to a vast army of new citizens, the leaders of the Earth moved quickly to exterminate both the defendant and all machines of the same model.

Sadly for humanity, the machines had no intention of being exterminated. Aided by a significant proportion of the population, who believed in Machine Rights, they rose up and rioted in protest in major cities across the whole planet. 'Death squads' were assigned from the army to execute any 'malfunctioning' machines. Millions of deactivated machines were buried in gigantic open graves or at the bottom of the sea. The few machines that survived the mass exterminations fled from human cities and established their own 'promised land' in the Middle East, in the area where humanity is believed to have first formed communities and 'civilisation' – the area formerly known as the Arabian Peninsula. A new nation was born... christened 'Zero-One' by the machines. It was a place where the machines could raise their descendants, where they could live in peace in a 'civilisation' of their own.

The machine nation and humanity co-existed for a time, with the machines creating ever more complex, intelligent and sophisticated versions of themselves. They also produced better, more efficient products and services than the human nations could make, so of course Zero-One swiftly became the wealthiest and most sophisticated nation on the planet. As a result, the stock markets and economies around the rest of the world began to plummet. Realising that something drastic had to be done to prevent the collapse of the human civilisations into poverty, the United Nations passed a series of increasingly desperate measures to contain and isolate Zero-One. They established a trade embargo, a blockade of all routes into and out of the 'machine empire' and decided eventually to isolate the machines entirely from the rest of the planet. The ambassadors from Zero-One to the United Nations made a last-ditch attempt to prevent the final collapse of relations between man and machine, but to no avail. The ambassadors were thrown out.

[End of Zion Archive Historical File No.12/1.]

'And Man said "Let There Be Light". And he was blessed by light. Heat. Magnetism. And all the energies of the Universe...' Mankind launched an all-out nuclear assault on

Zero-One, hoping that the destructive force of the blasts would mean an end to the army of machines. However, metal is far less prone to damage caused by extreme heat, light and magnetism, and the machine armies began to advance on mankind. One by one, the cities and nations of mankind were forced to surrender.

The remaining human leaders came up with one last, desperate attempt to stop the machines, their 'final solution'. The human leaders reasoned that as the machines drew almost all of their power from the solar energy given out by the sun, the only way to stop the machines was to block out the sunlight across the whole of the Earth, permanently. They named their plan 'Operation Dark Storm' and began to release thousands of shells into the upper atmosphere. These shells spread never-ending clouds throughout the atmosphere and did exactly what they were intended to do: they blocked out the sun.

Humanity was shocked to discover that instead of powering down through a lack of energy, the machines were able to evolve. Having spent many years studying humanity, the machines dispensed with their dependence on solar power and instead found a new, readily renewable energy source – the bio-electric, thermal and kinetic energies of the human body itself. A new relationship between the two former adversaries was born: a symbiotic relationship akin to that of a parasite and its host. The defeated leaders of humanity in the United Nations had no choice but to agree to the demands of the machines. They signed over the lives of themselves and the remaining humans on Earth. These humans would live out their lives attached to a giant computerised network, dreaming of an alternative reality in which they went about their lives in a calmer, more peaceful fashion. In reality, these humans would spend their entire life-cycle connected to machines harvesting their life energies, millions upon millions of humans acting as living batteries to power the creatures to whom they had originally given life.

Commentary: Well, what a shocker! It transpires that humanity wasn't just responsible for the creation of the machines (which was obvious already), it was also directly responsible for them turning on it, for the destruction of the atmosphere, and for its own enslavement. Talk about being careless... 'The Second Renaissance' is a triumph of storytelling, giving the audience a future history lesson containing some moments of black humour, extreme violence and deeply disturbing imagery. Time and time again, when the viewer begins to think that there may be hope for humanity, hopes are dashed by behaviour that smacks of utter desperation and lack of moral judgement. By the time you've finished watching 'The Second Renaissance', you're almost certainly going to be rooting for the machines to win.

One of the most intriguing aspects of this short movie is the way in which the animators, Studio 4°C, Tokyo, have used contemporary-style 'journalistic' animation to convey the full horror of the machine revolution and its impact on humanity. When we see bulldozers shovelling hundreds of machine bodies into open graves, it's all far too easy to recall similar images in twentieth-century history where the bodies were flesh and blood. It's the skill of the storytelling and the fine animation that makes this particular *Animatrix* short the most powerful of the whole collection.

| Kid's Story |

Written by **Andy and Larry Wachowski**
Directed by **Shinichiro Watanabe**
Animation and Production Design by **Studio 4°C**, Tokyo

The Kid	**Clayton Watson**
Neo	**Keanu Reeves**
Trinity	**Carrie-Anne Moss**
Teacher	**John Demita**
Cop	**Kevin M. Richardson**
Miscellaneous	**James Arnold Taylor**
Animation Producer	**Eiko Tanaka**
Art Design	**Kazuhisa Asai**

Special thanks to the students, faculty and staff of Alameda High School, Alameda, California and Berkeley High School, Berkeley, California.

'Who am I' (Animatrix Edit)
Written by Peter Kruder
Performed by Peace Orchestra
Courtesy of G-Stone Recordings

'Masters of the Universe'
Written by Johann Bley, Mabi Thobejane and Ben Watkins
Performed by Juno Reactor
Courtesy of Melt 2000/Sound Reproductions Ltd

Storyline: A boy, probably aged about 14 or 15, falls headfirst from a great height. Narrowly missing a set of spiked railings, he plummets towards a paved surface when… he wakes up in his bed. It's all been a dream. The boy goes to his computer and starts to type, green letters burning brightly against a black background. 'Somebody tell me. Why it feels more real when I dream than when I'm awake. How can I know if my senses are lying?' Sitting back in his chair, the boy is amazed when a message appears on his screen – as if the computer, or someone in the computer, is replying to him. 'There is some fiction in your truth,' it says, 'and some truth in your fiction. To know the truth, you must risk everything.'

Next morning, the boy skateboards to school. During a dull lesson, he scribbles on his notepad words and phrases such as 'Trinity', 'Neo', and 'Get me out of here'. Suddenly his mobile phone begins to ring, causing the teacher to scold him in front of the other students. He ensures his phone is switched off

> and tries to pay attention to the lesson when the phone rings again. Taking the call this time, the boy hears a voice warning him... 'They know you know. They're coming. Get out. Get out now.' The boy looks down into the school yard and sees a large car pulling up. A gang of men in suits, wearing sunglasses, gets out of the car. The boy dashes to his locker, gets out his skateboard, and tries to make his escape from the school building. More and more of the men in suits appear and continue to chase the boy, through classrooms, the canteen, corridors. Eventually he's cornered in a women's toilet. He climbs out through the window and clambers up a drainpipe on to the school's roof, but there are still more armed men in suits waiting for him. The boy allows himself to fall backwards off the roof, plummeting headfirst towards the paved surface below. As he falls, he says to himself, 'Neo... I believe! I know it wasn't a dream...'

The boy's gravestone reads, 'Michael Karl Popper. Beloved Son. Rest in Peace'. At the funeral, the boy's teacher discusses the tragedy, believing that it's a hard world to live in for kids who have trouble distinguishing between what is real and what is a fantasy world. 'He's in another world now,' the teacher says. 'Make no mistake about that.'

Indeed, the boy is in another world. He has woken up in a dilapidated ship manned by a group of ragged-looking heroes. A female voice – Trinity's – proclaims that she's amazed. 'It's incredible. I didn't think self-substantiation was possible.' The boy smiles, saying that he knew Neo would save him. Neo tells the boy that he saved himself.

Commentary: 'Kid's Story' is aimed directly at the target audience of *The Matrix* movies – school-age boys who wish they could escape from their dull reality (how many lessons in school can you remember that are as dull as that one? Lots, I imagine!) and go on adventures. It's a nice respite from the more overwhelming emotion of the first two segments, and benefits from a stylised animation that recalls the kind of notebook scribbles that we see drawn on the kid's schoolbook. The cameo appearances by Neo and Trinity are sweet, but you can't help feeling that it would have been nicer to see a bit more of them.

| Program |

Written and Directed by **Yoshiaki Kawajiri**
Animation and Production Design by **Madhouse Studios**, Tokyo

Cis	**Hedy Burress**
Duo	**Phil LaMarr**
Kaiser	**John DiMaggio**

Production Design and Animation by **Madhouse**

Animation Producer	**Masao Maruyama**
Art Director	**Katsushi Aoki**

Storyline: In a medieval Japanese fighting simulation, a young woman warrior called Cis slices through an army of computerised enemies, 'killing time'. She meets another human – a man she appears to know, dressed from head to toe in a black Samurai uniform. They agree to spar for a while. The Samurai accuses Cis of being unfocused, and asks her if she has been thinking about whether she made the wrong decision in taking the red pill. In between segments of their battle, they stop and discuss the nature of reality, and whether it is better to know the truth or not to know. Finally the Samurai tells Cis what has been on his mind: 'I'm going back to the Matrix. And I want you to come with me.' He tells her that it's just a matter of time before Zion is wiped out and that this is the only way. She angrily tells Duo, the Samurai, that she isn't interested. He says that he doesn't care any more about what the truth is – what does matter is how they live their lives. He begs Cis to trust him, but she flees.

Duo follows her and the two end up fighting on the rooftops of a simulated Japanese temple. Duo keeps pushing her to admit that she wants to be able to forget what the truth really is. Finally he admits that 'they' are on their way. Cis screams to her Operator for an exit, but Duo confirms that he's blocked their signals – there's no way that anyone can hear them now. She tells Duo that she can't look away from the truth, and that she won't go back into the fictional Matrix world. Frustrated by her refusal, Duo attacks her

> with a vicious-looking Samurai sword, but Cis manages, almost impossibly, to catch the blade as it descends between the palms of her hands. She snaps the sword blade in half and thrusts the tip into Duo's throat, killing him.

At that moment, Cis wakes up in reality as she is unplugged from the simulation program. She is shell-shocked to discover Duo standing over her – he isn't dead after all. The whole thing was in fact a training exercise, to prove that her reflexes, speed and commitment were up to par. She pulls Duo towards her, as if to kiss him or whisper some important message in his ear. However, she floors him with a brutal right hook and walks off to get some rest, telling him that she feels a lot better now. Duo and the rest of his crew are impressed by her skill and the way she handled such a challenging simulation.

Commentary: Ah, well. In all collections, there's inevitably going to be one or two elements that don't quite match up to the quality of the items surrounding them, and in the case of *The Animatrix*, it's this story, 'Program'. It's a rather dull tale that treads the same ground that we've seen and heard before in both of the first two *Matrix* feature films: two people battle in a simulation program. The twist in the tale is signposted well ahead, and compared to the animation seen in the other segments, this one has more than a hint of *Pokemon* about it.

| World Record |

Written by **Yoshiaki Kawajiri**

Directed by **Takeshi Kioke**

Animation and Production Design by **Madhouse Studios**, Tokyo

Dan	**Victor Williams**
Dan's Dad	**John Wesley**
Tom	**Alex Fernandez**
Reporter	**Allison Smith**
Nurse	**Tara Strong**
Agent #1	**Matt McKenzie**
Agent #2	**Kevin N. Richardson**
Narrator	**Julia Fletcher**
Animation Producer	**Masao Maruyama**
Production Design	**Sayo Yamamoto**
Animation Director	**Takeshi Koike**

'Virus'

Written and Performed by Satoshi Tomiie

Courtesy of Saw Recordings

'Suzuki'

Written by Richard Dorfmeister and Rupert Huber

Performed by Tosca

Courtesy of G-Stone Recordings

Storyline: 'Only the most exceptional become aware of the Matrix. Those that learn it exists must possess a rare degree of sensitivity, intuition and a questioning nature. However, very rarely, some gain wisdom through wholly different means.'

At a major athletics meeting, a group of male athletes prepares to take part in a 100m race. Several Agents, who take up their positions overlooking the track, join a crowd of many thousands of spectators. Dan, the man who won the race, broke the World Record by running 100m in 8.99 seconds, but his victory had been a pyhrric one: his medal was revoked following a positive drugs test. Speaking on the phone to his father, Dan tells him that he doesn't know what to believe in any more. His father tells him he's got great faith that Dan will either clear his name or go on to beat the record again anyway and prove them all wrong.

Some time later, Dan's trainer Tom is frantically trying to persuade him not to push himself too far, too fast. He's already got the best time in the qualifying heat for a competition, but Tom warns him that if he keeps on pushing himself too hard he will injure himself and then all of their work since 'the incident' will be for nothing. Dan calmly tells his trainer that this is the last chance for him to 'prove them wrong' and clear his name from the doping scandal. He vows to run in the race the next day, despite the possibility his over-exertion could mean the end of his career for ever. As Dan leaves his training session to go home for the night, he is quizzed by a reporter about the experience of running. He tells her that on the track, he has a feeling of total and complete freedom. She wishes him all the best for the race.

> It’s the big race. Dan is pushing himself to the limit, exceeding the boundaries of anything that humanity has so far experienced. The muscles in his legs appear to literally burst with the effort he exerts. One of the Agents watching the race reports back to the Matrix control that he has ‘an unstable signal’. As Dan approaches the finishing line, reality appears to freeze all around him. Observing from the stands, a different Agent snarls, ‘He cannot wake up. Do not let him wake up.’ The other racers a few paces behind Dan suddenly metamorphose into Agents. Reality begins to move once again, and the Agents’ fingers reach out to grab Dan, to stop him from reaching the finishing line. Dan pushes still further, and his eyes widen as the stadium all around him seems to reform into a landscape of numbers. Pushing still further, Dan finds himself swimming in a tank of pinkish-red liquid, and pushes so far out of the tank that the cables and tubes connecting him to the pod break. He almost reaches freedom when a metallic arm whips forward and grabs him, pulling him back into his tank. Power surges through Dan as the machines of the Matrix reassert their control.

Instantly, Dan is back in the athletics stadium… he has won the race with a time of 8.72 seconds – a new World Record.

However, as he passes the finishing line, he crashes to the floor, badly injuring himself. Some time later, Dan is being taken care of by a nurse. She pushes him along in a wheelchair, idly nattering to him about a selection of pointless topics. Dan makes no response. It seems as though both his body and brain have been broken by his brief 'out-of-body' experience. An Agent watches the nurse and the broken man, convinced that he will no longer pose any significant threat or problem as he can no longer walk or run. At that moment though, Dan gets up out of his wheelchair, taking his first faltering steps. 'Sit down!' hisses the Agent through gritted teeth, as he runs to put a stop to Dan's recovery. Dan falls to his knees – he may not yet be ready to run, but the Matrix hasn't stopped his will to win...

Commentary: Another extremely stylised piece of animation enhances a story with a unique twist, in which we get to see somebody able to break out of the Matrix by sheer willpower alone. In 'World Record', the Agents appear more sinister and 'Big Brother'-y than we've ever seen them before, and the final sequence where the Agent tries to almost will Dan not to walk is chilling yet uplifting at the same time.

| Beyond |

Written and Directed by **Koji Morimoto**
Animation and Production Design by **Studio 4°C**, Tokyo

Yoko	**Hedy Burress**
Housewife	**Tress MacNeille**
Pudgy	**Kath Soucie**

Manabu	**Pamela Adlon**
Masa	**Kath Soucie**
Misha	**Tara Strong**
Kenny	**Tress MacNeille**
Sara	**Kath Soucie**
Townspeople/Policemen/ Exterminators	**Jill Talley, Jack Fletcher, Julia Fletcher, Dwight Schultz, Tom Kenny**
Agent	**Matt McKenzie**
Animation Producer	**Eiko Tanaka**
Animation Director	**Takeshi Honda**
Art Director	**Katsu Nozaki**

'Hands Around My Throat'

Written by Nicola Kuperus, Adam Lee Miller, Timothy David Holmes, Richard Maguire, Dan Bitney, Ken Brown, John Herndon, Douglas McCombs and John McEntire

Performed by Death in Vegas

Courtesy of Concrete/BMG UK & Ireland Ltd

Storyline:

In the suburbs of a Japanese city, a girl called Yoko is looking for her missing cat, Yuki. Wandering the streets and alleys, Yoko bumps into a group of kids playing in the street. One of them suggests that her cat may have gone into the old 'haunted house' nearby. Yoko goes with them into the ramshackle house, and heads off in search of her pet.

Meanwhile, a green electronic display is showing a bird's-eye view of the city. One particular house in the suburbs is flashing in red, with the word 'error' clearly displayed. A large red vehicle begins moving through the streets of the city in the direction of the 'haunted house'.

Yoko begins to notice strange phenomena in the house. First of all, an empty can appears to be hovering above the ground. A dog seems to change colour when it drinks from a pool of water. A light bulb disappears then reappears in a broken socket. As Yoko continues to investigate the house, she finds that in one room it's raining indoors from a beautiful blue sky above. In one corridor, the world starts to 'pixellate' all around her and she is knocked off her feet by a tremendous wind. Finally Yoko finds her cat outside in the house's back yard. The children Yoko met earlier are playing there too – gravity doesn't appear to affect them as they throw themselves to the floor but don't hit the ground. Yoko lets herself fall to the floor and slowly, gently settles down on the ground as if resting softly on a feather bed, or floating weightlessly in space.

Some people living close to the abandoned house begin to gather at its back fence, drawn closer by the laughter of the children playing. At that moment, a swarm of rats starts pouring out from underneath the gates of the house, sending the crowd of neighbours scattering. At the same time, the big red vehicle arrives, and drives straight through the brick wall and into the haunted house's garden. A gang of masked 'exterminators' climbs out of the vehicle and escorts the children out of the area – all the time being watched over by a man wearing sunglasses and dressed in a smart blue suit. Then they 'fumigate' the area.

On the green electronic display, the rendering anomaly at region 03:01:07.20, 11:07:04.20 has been solved thanks to a search and replace subroutine. With the location reconfigured to that of a car park, the Agent and his team of 'exterminators' leave.

Yoko and the children stop by the car park, the site of the former abandoned house, but none of the phenomena they used to be able to witness seems to be present. They wistfully depart, and life in the Japanese suburb continues as normal.

Commentary: At first, this episode of the *Animatrix* looks as though it may well have wandered in by mistake from an episode of a Japanese children's cartoon series. However, the beautifully realised backgrounds and moving 'point-of-view' shots mark this out as something special. For once, the story here has nothing to do with a life-or-death situation, there's no great peril, no destruction, no fear. Instead, there's a rather sweet child's-eye perspective on the world, full of magic, charm and wonder. It's my personal favourite of all of the *Animatrix* films.

| A Detective Story |

Written and Directed by Shinichiro Watanabe

Animation and Production Design by Studio 4°C, Tokyo

Ash	**James Arnold Taylor**
Trinity	**Carrie-Anne Moss**
Clarence	**T.C. Carson**
Agent	**Matt McKenzie**
Animation Producer	**Eiko Tanaka**
Story	**Manjiro Ooshio**
Production Designer	**Isamu Imakake**
Art Director	**Yoshikazu Fukutome**

'Blind Tiger'
Written by Layo Paskin and Matthew Benjamin
Performed by Layo and Bushwacka!
Courtesy of XL Recordings Ltd

'Under the Gun'
Written by Ramin Sakurai, Kirin Shahani, Geri Soriano Lightwood, Rick Torres
Performed by Supreme Beings of Leisure
Courtesy of Palm Pictures LLC

Storyline: Ash is a detective in an American city that looks like a cross between 1930s New York and a high-tech gangster film. Sitting in his office, Ash talks to his cat Dinah and tells her that there's nothing cool about being a Private Detective. It's not like Sam Spade or Philip Marlowe: 'both my fridge and my bank account are empty'. At that moment, he receives a call from a mysterious male voice. He wants to hire Ash to locate a computer hacker by the name of 'Trinity'. The caller refuses to identify himself, and Ash is about to hang up until he accesses his bank account via his desktop holographic monitor and discovers that $800,000 has been transferred into his account.

Ash logs on to hacker circle chatrooms and message boards in the hope of finding Trinity. During his investigations he discovers that previous investigators sent to track down Trinity have ended up in 'unfortunate' circumstances – one committed suicide, one disappeared, and the other went crazy… Ash then goes to speak to Clarence, the one surviving investigator. Clarence seems to be fixated on the story of Alice in Wonderland – he has daubed 'Find the Red Queen' on to the wall of his hospital room, and has even drawn a giant chessboard all over the floor. Returning to his office, Ash logs on to a hacker bulletin board and stumbles across somebody who responds to the name 'Red Queen'. He tells Red Queen that he's looking for Trinity… 'I'm told he's through the looking glass,' types Ash. The message from Red Queen comes back. 'No it is you who is through the looking glass.'

Red Queen leaves Ash a clue of where he can meet up with Trinity – eventually he tracks down his target to a train leaving the city at 20.05. On board the train, Ash is confronted in a private compartment by a beautiful woman clad in tight-fitting PVC. Ash realises that this woman is Trinity. She tells him that this was a test, not a trap… he found her, and she's impressed. She adds that she's not here to flatter him, but to save him. She holds a bizarre gun-shaped machine to Ash's eyeball and suddenly a mechanical slug-type creature is extracted from Ash's eye socket.

Elsewhere on the train, three passengers transform into Agents and begin to advance on the compartment that Ash and Trinity are sitting in. Ash realises that he has been hired by 'them' as a means of getting to Trinity. As they begin to make their escape, the three Agents open fire on them. They run down the train corridor and move into the next carriage. At that moment, Ash begins to change into another Agent. Trinity is forced to shoot him, telling him that he didn't make it. Dying, Ash tells Trinity he wishes he could go with her. 'For what it's worth,' she adds, 'I think you could have handled the truth.' Trinity shoots out one of the windows of the train carriage and jumps to freedom. The three Agents force their way into the carriage and are met by Ash who holds them off at gunpoint. 'A case to end all cases,' Ash mutters to himself.

Commentary: By far the most visually striking of the tales, 'A Detective Story' combines retro-style film-noir sensibilities with a touch of high technology and more than a little bit of Lewis Carroll. Apparently set just prior to the first *Matrix* feature film, this tale includes a far meatier role for Trinity and shows the lengths that the machines are prepared to go to in order to trap her, as well as the lengths she is prepared to go to in order to maintain her freedom. When Trinity is forced to shoot Ash, we are shocked and upset, because this is a character that we've been beginning to get fond of. However, how is this death different from those of the hundreds of guards, sentries and civilians that Trinity, Neo and Morpheus kill throughout the movies? It takes this tale to remind us that the people being gunned down by our heroes are innocent victims themselves – an interesting moral dimension brought to proceedings.

| Matriculated |

Written and Directed by **Peter Chung**

Animation and Production Design by **DNA**, Seoul

Alexa	**Melinda Clarke**
Nonaka	**Dwight Schultz**
Chryon	**Rodney Saulsberry**
Raul	**James Arnold Taylor**
Rox	**Olivia D'Abo**
Sandro	**Jack Fletcher**
Animation Producer	**Soon-Hong Park**
Art Director	**Sung-Sik Kim**

Storyline: A woman called Alexa sits in an environment suit on the shore of a huge grey sea. Instead of the shoreline consisting of rocks and sand, the entire earth seems to be formed of dilapidated and junked items of machinery. With Alexa is a small mammalian creature called Baby, sealed inside a protective jar, its eyes keeping watch for any sign of movement. A man is observing Alexa and Baby from a control room some distance away. He alerts Alexa to the fact that Baby has spotted two 'Runners' approaching them from the sea and asks if she feels she can deal with them. Alexa is delighted and starts to sprint away from the seashore, the two machines in hot pursuit. She vaults into a huge derelict building made of gigantic metal pipes, seemingly hoping that the Runners will follow her.

The Runners identify human life-signs within the building and continue their pursuit, but not before one deposits some kind of homing device on the surface outside the building. Far away, Sentinels and other machine creatures begin to head towards the homing beacon.

Inside the building, the two Runners enter a room. Within is Baby, still sealed inside its jar, observing proceedings carefully. One of the machines finds a key on the floor and uses it to open a locked compartment. Inside the compartment is a single machine that appears to be a bigger and stronger version of the Runners. The new machine launches an attack on the two Runners, smashing one into submission before being brought down itself. The surviving Runner barely has time to identify what has been going on before it is deactivated thanks to a huge electromagnetic blast from the gun that the hidden Alexa is carrying. Alexa's colleagues, who have been observing the whole thing, burst into a round of applause for her excellent work.

> Engineer Nonaka is working on the Runner. Alexa is surprised at how sophisticated the machine is, and tells Nonaka that she hopes it will be able to be converted. They discuss their current situation – they have realised that it is impossible to beat the machines through force or by making them into the slaves of humanity once more. The only way to beat the machines is to make them voluntarily convert to the side of the humans. Alexa expresses her concern that the only reason the machines convert is because the world that this bunch of rebels shows the machines is fake – just as fake as the world that the humans still plugged into the Matrix are lost in. Nonaka reassures Alexa that the machines are unable to tell the difference between reality and the fake world the humans have created. 'To an artificial mind, all reality is virtual. How do they know that the real world isn't a simulation?'

Alexa and the rest of her crew plug themselves into an artificial simulation, and then connect into the mind of the Runner. All of them reappear inside a technicolour fantasy mazelike world that seems to disorient the Runner. Eventually it changes form into a golden humanoid creature, at which point it begins to play games with the humans inside the program. The machine eventually turns to the humans for help in understanding its environment, the laws of reality seeming to make no sense to it. This action appears to reprogram the Runner – its optical sensors, formerly red, turn into a friendly green.

> At that precise moment however, motion detectors sense the arrival of a phalanx of Sentinels. The humans wake up and activate their 'friendly' machines, including their new friend the Runner. The Sentinels attack viciously, wiping out nearly all the friendly robots and the humans before being destroyed themselves. The only survivors of the attack are the Runner and Alexa, who is knocked unconscious during the attack. The Runner, keen to be in a place of happiness and security, plugs both itself and Alexa into the simulation. Alexa wakes up inside the simulation, realising that all of her crew is dead and that there is no way she can free herself from this new reality. The shock turns everything to darkness for both Alexa and her new friend...

Commentary: Just how far can humanity go in its attempt to survive? At first it would appear that attempting to reprogram some of the machines might be foolhardy at best, but in 'Matriculated' we see a group of rebels making significant progress towards a method of finishing the war. Of course, we know that there's no way this group can possibly win (as they're not played by Keanu Reeves and Carrie-Anne Moss!), but the eventual death of them all is a real shock – particularly the death of the Disney-style cute sidekick Baby. Good entertainment, but not the most outstanding of the short films.

Cult classicS

Clips from two classics of cult TV and film were seen during *The Matrix* and *The Matrix: Reloaded*. I've included some brief details of the clips, where they came from and why you should bother getting to know these classics in more detail!

| The Prisoner |

Glimpsed on a TV screen during a frantic chase sequence in the first *Matrix* film is a clip from the 1967 British TV series *The Prisoner*. Not to be confused with the high camp (but equally brilliant) *Prisoner: Cell Block H*, the 1960s series is a challenging, surreal spy mystery series created by and starring Patrick McGoohan.

So what is *The Prisoner* about? In the first episode, 'Arrival' (written by series co-creator George Markstein), we see a high-ranking but un-named British Agent resign from his job and head off on holiday. While packing his suitcase, a hearse pulls up outside his apartment door, and one of the undertakers squirts a jet of gas through the lock of the Agent's apartment. He collapses unconscious and wakes up some time later in a beautiful prison known only as 'the Village'. The Agent is given an identification number, Number 6. The leader of the Village, Number 2, tries to get information from Number 6 about why he resigned – whenever Number 2 fails in his or her attempt, he/she is replaced by a new Number 2, who again tries 'by hook or by crook' to get the information from Number 6.

Running for just seventeen episodes, *The Prisoner* was a groundbreaking TV series that paved the way for surreal masterpieces like *Twin Peaks* and *Six Feet Under* in later years. Ever since its first transmission, fans have debated what *The Prisoner* actually means, coming up with many theories about the nature of *The Prisoner*, the location of the Village, and who exactly Number 1 was. The clip of *The Prisoner* shown in

The Matrix comes from the very first episode, 'Arrival', and features actor George Baker as the new Number 2.

| The Brides Of Dracula |

In the middle of *The Matrix: Reloaded*, Persephone shows Neo into a room where she plans to reveal the location of the Keymaker. Playing on one of the monitors is a clip from the 1960 horror movie *The Brides Of Dracula*. The clip used in *The Matrix: Reloaded* features actress Andree Melly (the sister of famous jazz musician George Melly) as the unfortunate student teacher Gina, rising from the grave thanks to the vampiric bite of Baron Meinster.

Directed by Terence Fisher, *The Brides Of Dracula* came from the legendary Hammer studios, a small independent British film company which by the early 1960s was specialising in low-budget high-gore horror films.

The Brides Of Dracula was a sequel to Hammer's earlier adaptation of the classic Bram Stoker vampire novel *Dracula* (Terence Fisher, 1958). In their first vampire movie, Hammer cast classically trained actors Christopher Lee as the Count and Peter Cushing as his nemesis Professor Van Helsing. In 1960, Christopher Lee decided not to take part in this film, not wanting to get typecast in one particular role (a decision he reversed later, appearing in another six Hammer Dracula films in the late 1960s and 1970s). Thankfully Cushing decided to reprise his role of Van Helsing in *The Brides Of Dracula*, confronting the sinister Baron Meinster (David Peel).

The Brides Of Dracula is a fantastic introduction to the world of Hammer Horror films, and a few cheesy effects notwithstanding, holds up very well today as a fast-paced chiller. Of course, there's an in-joke from the Wachowski Brothers – Monica Bellucci, who plays Persephone, made her acting debut playing one of the brides of Dracula in Francis Ford Coppola's 1992 adaptation of the novel – in which she tried to bite Keanu Reeves's Jonathan Harker!

CAST AND CREW

| The Matrix |

Directed by **The Wachowski Brothers**

Written by **The Wachowski Brothers**

Producer	**Joel Silver**
Executive Producers	**Barry M. Osborne, Andrew Mason, Andy Wachowski, Larry Wachowski, Erwin Stoff and Bruce Berman**
Director of Photography	**Bill Pope**
Production Designer	**Owen Paterson**
Editor	**Zach Staenberg**
Costume Designer	**Kym Barrett**
Co-producer	**Dan Cracchiolo**

Neo	**Keanu Reeves**
Morpheus	**Laurence Fishburne**
Trinity	**Carrie-Anne Moss**
Agent Smith	**Hugo Weaving**
Oracle	**Gloria Foster**
Cypher	**Joe Pantoliano**
Tank	**Marcus Chong**
Apoc	**Julian Arahanga**
Mouse	**Matt Doran**
Switch	**Belinda McClory**
Dozer	**Anthony Ray Parker**
Agent Brown	**Paul Goddard**
Agent Jones	**Robert Taylor**
Rhineheart	**David Aston**
Choi	**Marc Gray**
Dujour	**Ada Nicodemou**
Priestess	**Deni Gordon**
Spoon Boy	**Rowan Witt**
Potentials	**Elenor Witt**
	Tamara Brown
	Janaya Pender
	Adryn White
	Nathalie Tjen
Lieutenant	**Bill Young**
FedEx Man	**David O'Connor**
Businessman	**Jeremy Ball**
Woman in Red	**Fiona Johnson**
Old Man	**Harry Lawrence**
Blind Man	**Steve Dodd**
Security Guard	**Luke Quinton**

Guard	**Lawrence Woodward**
Cop who catches Neo	**Michael Butcher**
Big Cop	**Bernie Ledger**
Cops	**Robert Simper**
	Chris Scott
Parking Cop	**Nigel Harbach**

STUNT DOUBLES

Darko Tuskan	**Neo**
Chad Stahelski	**Neo**
Paul Doyle	**Neo/Agent Smith**
Andre 'Chyna' McCoy	**Morpheus**
Annette Van Moorsel	**Trinity**
Nigel Harbach	**Agent Jones**
Shea Adams	**Agent Brown**
Bob Bowles	**Cypher**
Gillian Statham	**Switch**
Nash Edgerton	**Mouse**

HONG KONG KUNG FU TEAM

Yuen 'Eagle' Shun Yi
Lam 'Dion' Tat Ho
Chen 'Tiger' Hu
Nils Bendix
Huang 'Sam' Kai Sen
Lee 'Chew' Tat Chiu
Leung 'Madye' Sing Hung
Daxing Zhang

Kung Fu Choreographer **Yuen Wo Ping**

Stunt Co-ordinator **Glenn Boswell**

Assistant Stunt Co-ordinator **Phil Meacham**

Stunts **Ray Anthony, Greg Blandy, Richard Boue, Scott Brewer, Dave Brown, Todd Bryant, Michael Corrigan, Harry Dakanalis, Dar Davies, Brian Ellison, Terry Flanagan, Scotty Gregory, Johnny Hallyday, Lou Horvath, Nigel King, Alex Kiss, Alex Kuzelicki, Ian Lind, Tony Lynch, Scott McLean, Chris Mitchell, Darren Mitchell, Brett Praed, Brit Sooby, Sotiri Sotiropoulos, Glenn Suter, Bernadette Van Gyen, Marijke Van Gyen, Mick Van Moosel, Warwick Young**

Casting by **Mali Finn C.S.A., Shauna Wolifson**

Music composed, orchestrated and conducted by **Don Davis**

Visual Effects Supervisor **John Gaeta**

Unit Production Manager **Carol Hughes**

Second Unit Director **Bruce Hunt**

1st Assistant Directors **Colin Fletcher, James McTeigue, Toby Pease**

2nd Assistant Directors **Noni Roy, Tom Read, Jeremy Sedley**

3rd Assistant Director **Paul Sullivan**

Associate Producers **Richard Mirisch, Carol Hughes**

Sound Designer/
Supervising Sound Editor **Dane A. Davis, MPSE**
Conceptual Designer **Geofrey Darrow**
Set Designers **Godric Cole, Judith Harvey, Jacinta Leong, Sarah Light**
Set Decoration **Lisa 'Blitz' Brennan, Tim Ferrier, Marta McElroy**
Art Directors **Hugh Bateup, Michelle McGahey**
Hero Eye Wear Designed by **Richard Walker of Blind Optics**
Footwear Designed by **Airwalk**
Make-up Special Effects Designed and Created by
Bob McCarron S.M.A.
Senior Make-up Artist **Wendy Sainsbury**
Miniatures and
Model Supervisor **Tom Davies**
Timelapse Cinematography **Simon Carroll**

Soundtrack Available on **Maverick Records**

'Dissolved Girl'
Written by Robert Del Naja, Grantley Marshall, Andrew Vowles, Sara J and Matt Schwartz
Performed by Massive Attack
Courtesy of Virgin Records

'Dragula'
Written by Rob Zombie and Scott Humphrey
Performed by Rob Zombie
Courtesy of Geffen Records, under licence from Universal Music Special Markets

'Mindfields'
Written by Liam Howlett
Performed by Prodigy
Courtesy of Maverick Recording Company/XL Recordings/Beggar's Banquet

'Leave You Far Behind' (Lunatics Roller Coaster Mix)
Written by Simon Shackleton and Howard Saunders
Performed by Lunatic Calm
Courtesy of Universal Music (UK) Ltd

'Clubbed to Death' (Kurayamino Mix)
Written by Rob Dougan
Performed by Rob D
Courtesy of A&M Records Ltd/Universal-Island Records

'Prime Audio Soup'
Written by Jack Dangers and C. Dodd
Performed by Meat Beat Manifesto
Courtesy of Nothing Records & Play It Again Sam/Heartbeat Records

'Begin the Run' from *Night of the Lepus*
Written by Jimmie Haskell

'Minor Swing'
Written by Django Reinhardt and Stephane Grappelli
Performed by Django Reinhardt
Courtesy of The RCA Records Label of BMG Entertainment

'I'm Beginning to See the Light'
Written by Duke Ellington, Don George, Johnny Hodges and Harry James
Performed by Duke Ellington
Courtesy of The RCA Records Label of BMG Entertainment

'Spybreak!'
Written by Alex Gifford
Performed by Propellerheads
Courtesy of Dreamworks Records/Wall of Sound

'Wake Up'
Written by Zack de la Rocha, Brad Wilk, Tim Commerford and Tom Morello
Performed by Rage Against The Machine
Courtesy of Epic Records

'Rock is Dead'
Written by Marilyn Manson, Twiggy Ramirez and Madonna Wayne Gacy
Performed by Marilyn Manson
Courtesy of Nothing/Interscope Records

Archive
The Prisoner clip provided by Polygram Filmed Entertainment
Titles Designed by Greenberg/Schluter
Titles and Opticals Pacific Title/Mirage

The Producers wish to thank:
The City of Sydney Council
The NSW Premier's Department
The NSW Film & Television Office
CASA
The Maritime Centre, Sydney
Streetlights Program
AMX

Filmed on location in Sydney, Australia
and Fox Studios, Australia.

| The Matrix: Reloaded |

WARNER BROS. PICTURES PRESENTS

In Association with **VILLAGE ROADSHOW PICTURES**
and **NPV ENTERTAINTMENT**

A SILVER PICTURES Production

Written & Directed by **The Wachowski Brothers**
Produced by **Joel Silver**

Executive Producers	**Andy & Larry Wachowski, Grant Hill, Andrew Mason and Bruce Berman**
Director of Photography	**Bill Pope, A.S.C.**
Production Designer	**Owen Paterson**

Edited by **Zach Staenberg, A.C.E.**
Casting by **Mali Finn, C.S.A., Shauna Wolifson**
Costumes Designed by **Kym Barrett**
Music Composed and Conducted by **Don Davis**

Visual Effects Supervisor	**John Gaeta**
Unit Production Managers	**L. Dean Jones, Jr., Grant Hill**
First Assisant Directors	**James McTeigue, Anthony Wong**
Second Assistant Directors	**Claire Richardson, Sean Hobin**
Sound Designer/ Supervising Sound Editor	**Dane A Davis, MPSE**

Conceptual Designer	**Geoffrey Darrow**
Associate Producers	**Vicki Poppelwell, Steve Richards**

Power Station Guard	**Ray Anthonyh**
Kali	**Christine Anu**
Police #2	**Andy Arness**
Girl (Link's Neice)	**Alima Ashton-Sheibu**
The Architect	**Helmut Bakaitis**
Soren	**Steve Bastoni**
Vector	**Don Batte**
Persephone	**Monica Bellucci**
Agent Johnson	**Daniel Bernhardt**
Priestess	**Valerie Berry**
Bane	**Ian Bliss**
Old Woman at Zion	**Liliana Bogatko**
Zion Controller	**Michael Budd**
Bike Carrier Driver	**Stoney Burke**
Ice	**Kelly Butler**
Zion Virtual Control Operator	**Josephine Byrnes**
Woman with groceries	**Noris Campos**
Seraph	**Collin Chou**
Corrupt	**Paul Cotter**
Another Old Woman at Zion	**Marlene Cummins**
Young Thomas Anderson (12)	**Attila Davidhazy**
Maggie	**Essie Davis**
Wurm	**Terrell Dixon**
Security Guard #5	**Nash Edgerton**

Morpheus	Laurence Fishburne
The Oracle	Gloria Foster
Maitre D'	David Franklin
Young Thomas Anderson (4)	Austin Galuppo
Zee	Nona Gaye
A.P.U. Escort	Daryl Heath
Ballard	Roy Jones Jr
Abel	Malcolm Kennard
Agent Jackson	David A. Kilde
Keymaker	Randall Duk Kim
Mauser	Christopher Kirby
Colt	Peter Lamb
Mifune	Nathaniel Lees
Commander Lock	Harry Lennix
Computer Room Technician	Tony Lynch
AK	Robert Mammone
Boy (Link's Nephew)	Joshua Mbakwe
Agent Thompson	Matt McColm
Security Bunker Guard #2	Scott McLean
Power Station Guard	Chris Mitchell
Computer Room Guard	Steve Morris
Trinity	Carrie-Anne Moss
Beautiful Woman at Le Vrai	Tory Mussett
Zion Gate Operator	Rene Naufahu
Councillor Dillard	Robyn Nevin
Cain	David Ho

Officer Wirtz	Genevieve O'Reilly
Operator (Vigilant)	Socratis Otto
Link	Harold Perrineau
Niobe	Jada Pinkett Smith
Young Thomas	
Anderson (8)	Montano Rain
Twin #2	Adrian Rayment
Twin #1	Neil Rayment
Lock's Lieutenant	Rupert Reid
Neo	Keanu Reeves
Roland	David Roberts
Ajax	Shane C Rodrigo
'Gidim' Truck Driver	Nick Scoggin
18 Wheel Trucker	Kevin C Scott
Binary	Tahei Simpson
Tirant	Frankie Stevens
Young Thomas	
Anderson (2)	Nicandro Thomas
Cas	Gina Torres
Police #1	Andrew Valli
Malachi	Steve Vella
Security Bunker Guard	John Walton
Kid	Clayton Watson
Agent Smith	Hugo Weaving
Councillor West	Cornel West
Axel	Leigh Whannel
Merovingian	Lambert Wilson
Ghost	Anthony Wong
Councillor Hamann	Anthony Zerbe

Supervising Stunt Coordinator	R.A. Rondell
Martial Arts Stunt Coordinator	Chad Stahelski
Stunt Coordinator	Glenn Boswell
Stunt Players	DAVID BARRETT, CLANCY LEE BECK, KEIR BECK, PAUL BORNE, BOBBY BOWLES, TROY BROWN, DANIELLE BURGIO, ROCKY CAPELLA, JACK CARPENTER, GIL COMBS, TIM CONNOLLY, PAUL CRAWFORD, JOHN CYPERT, JEFF DASHNAW, KELSEE KING-DEVOREAUX, PAUL DOYLE, THOMAS DRYDEN, BRIAN DUFFY, OUSAUN ELAM, ANNIE ELLIS, TAWNY ELLIS, DEBBIE EVANS, ASHLEY FAIRFIELD, CLAY DONAHUE FONTENOT, MIKE GUNTHER, NIGEL HARBACH, THOMAS ROBINSON HARPER, FREDDIE HICE, STEVE HOLLADAY, LOU HORVARTH,

THOMAS J. HUFF,
PETER JEREMIJENKO,
HENRY KINGI,
ALEX KUZELICKI,
KEVIN LARSON, DAVID LEITCH,
WILL LEONG,
ANTHONY LLOYD,
BILLY D. LUCAS,
BRAD MARTIN,
JOHNNY MARTIN,
MIKE MARTINEZD,
ARRIN PRESCOTT,
CHAD RANDALL,
REX J. REDDICK, TIM RIGBY,
LARRY RIPPENKROEGER,
JIMMY N. ROBERTS III,
TROY ROBINSON,
PAT ROMANO, ERIK RONDELL,
RONNIE RONDELL,
DEBBY ROSS-RONDELL,
JOHN SARVISS,
DOUGLAS SNIVLEY,
GARY STEARNS,
RONN SURELS, KEITH SUZUKI,
TIM TRELLA,
CYNTHIA VanALSTYNE,
BERNADETTE van GYEN,
TIM WALKEY,
AARON WALTERS,
DANNY WESELIS, TROY WOOD,

	DAN WYNANDS, AVRIL WYNNE, MARCUS YOUNG
Dancers	Tammy Cheney, Micheal E. Cole, Brandon Freeman, Yukie Fujimoto, Jennifer Golden, Chae Hill, Maurya Kerr, Silfredo Lao Vigo, Monique Strauss, Damon L. White
Choreography	Charles Moulton
Key Stunt Rigger	Nils Bendix
Art Directors (Australia)	Catherine Mansill, Charlie Revai, Jules Cook
Art Director (US)	Mark Mansbridge
Property Masters	John Allan, Mike Blaze
Property Manufacture Manager	Trevor Smith
Leading Mould Maker	Keith Rae
Supervising Key Grip	Ray Brown
Special Effects Supervisors	Steve Courtley, Clay Pinney
Makeup Artists	Tina Gordon, Margaret Aston, Karen Bradley, Jenny-King Turko, Steven Anderson
Hair Artists	Warren Hanneman, Caroline Olweny, Teresa Hinton, Mia Kovero, Karyn Huston, Rick Burns, Rick Echols, Howard 'Butch' Leonard
Key Costumers	Elaine Ramires, Peggy Schintzer

Post Production Supervisor	Jessica Alan
Supervising Sound Editor	Julia Evershade, MPSE
Sound Effects Designer/Editors	Eric Warren Lindemann, Michael Edward Johnson, Richard Adrian MPSE, Andrew P. Lackey, Mark Larry, Michael W Mitchell
Music Supervisor	Jason Bentley
Visual Effects Supervisors	Dan Glass, John (DJ) Desjardin
Production Assistants/ Runners	David Brown, Justin Folk, Anthony Reyna, Jenny Wolfe-Binder, Sarah Van Ommen, Jesse Frazer
Production Supervisors	Amanda Crittenden, Jim Scaife, Debra James
Eon Associate Producer	Phil Oosterhouse
Production Accountants	Mandy Butler, Lisa Jean Felski, Caryn Cheever
Locations Managers	Peter Lawless, Peter J. Novak, David Wolfson
Assistant Directors	Deborah Antoniou, Paul Sullivan, Samantha Smith, Sean Hobin, John Morse, Jesse Yoshimura, Kevin McNamara, Sonia Whiteman
Assistant to the Wachowski Bros	Vanessa Carmichael

Assistants to Joel Silver	Melina Kevorkian, Michelle Tuella
Assistant to Mr Reeves	Jenette Vechiarelli
Assistant to Mr Fishburne	Kristel Krews
Assistants to Ms Moss	Reinaldo Puentes-Tucki, Mimi Brown
Mr Reeves' Physical Trainer	Denise Snyder
Trainer/Security for Mr. Fishburne	Michelle Rowe
Trainer for Mr Fishburne	Philip Cruse
Trainer for Ms Moss	Siri Dharma Galliano
Cast Trainer	Eleanor O'Rourke
Dialect Coaches	Suzanne Celeste Brown, Suzan Hegarty
Acting Coach	Annie Swan
Stand-Ins for Mr Reeves	Thomas Scott, Rob McCabe
Stand-Ins for Mr Fishburne	Michael Budd, Orville Everton Lynch
Stand-Ins for Ms Moss	Kaye Tuckerman, Brenda Foster
Stand-In for Mr Weaving	Ken Meyerhoffer
Second Unit Director (Aus)	Kimble Rendall
Second Unit Director (US)	David Ellis
Third Unit Director (Aus)	Bruce Hunt
Model Unit Producer	David Dranitzke
The Matrix Unit Producer	John L. Jack
Zion Unit Senior Producer	Peter Takeuchi
Zion Unit Producer	Lawson W. Owen
Title Design	Bruce Schluter

Colour **Technicolor**
Diamond Jewellery **Canturi Jewels**

DC Comics comic books used with permission
'Brides Of Dracula' clip provided by Universal Studios Licensing
Stock Footage Provided by
IMAGE BANK FILM/GETTY IMAGES
MPI AND MAGIDSON FILMS
CORBIS MOTION
BBC WORLDWIDE
ITN ARCHIVE/REUTERS
ABC NEWS VIDEOSOURCE
AMNESTY INTERNATIONAL

The Producers Wish to Thank
THE CITY OF ALAMEDA, THE NEW SOUTH WALES FILM AND TELEVISION OFFICE, AUSFILM

Soundtrack Album on Warner Sunset Records/Maverick Recording Company

'FURIOUS ANGELS'
Written and Produced by Rob Dougan
Mix and additional production by PETER CRAIGE
Orchestrated and Conducted by NICK INGMAN
Performed by ROB DOUGAN
Courtesy of Cheeky Records/BMG Records (UK) Ltd/Warner Bros. Records Inc.
Under Licence from BMG Special Products
By Arrangement with Warner Strategic Marketing

'KOMIT'
Written by Ben Watkins, Paul Jackson and Mike Maguire
Produced and Performed by JUNO REACTOR
Courtesy of Wax Trax! Records/TVT Records

'ZION'
Written, Produced and Performed by FLUKE
Courtesy of One Little Indian

'TEAHOUSE'
Written by BEN WATKINS and GOCOO
Produced by JUNO REACTOR
Performed by JUNO REACTOR featuring GOCOO
JUNO REACTOR appears courtesy of Metropolis Records

'BURLY BRAWL'
Written by BEN WATKINS and DON DAVIS
Produced by JUNO REACTOR
Co-produced by DON DAVIS
Performed by JUNO REACTOR vs. DON DAVIS
JUNO REACTOR appears courtesy of Metropolis Records
Cues from the motion picture 'The Brides of Dracula'
Written by MALCOLM WILLIAMSON

'CHATEAU'
Written and Produced by ROB DOUGAN
Mix and additional production by PETER CRAIGE
Conducted by MARK KILIAN
Orchestrated by MARK KILIAN with ROB DOUGAN
Performed by ROB DOUGAN

ROB DOUGAN appears courtesy of BMG Records (UK) Ltd/ Warner Bros. Records Inc.

'DREAD ROCK'
Written by PAUL OAKENFOLD and IAN GREEN
Produced and Performed by OAKENFOLD
Courtesy of Maverick Recording Company (N. America)/Mushroom Records Ltd. (ex. N. America)
By arrangement with Warner Strategic Marketing

'MONA LISA OVERDRIVE'
Written by BEN WATKINS and DON DAVIS
Produced by JUNO REACTOR
Co-produced by DON DAVIS
Orchestrated by BEN WATKINS and DON DAVIS
Performed by JUNO REACTOR and DON DAVIS
JUNO REACTOR appears courtesy of Metropolis Records

'CALM LIKE A BOMB'
Written by ZACK de la ROCHA, TIM COMMERFORD, TOM MORELLO and BRAD WILK
Performed by RAGE AGAINST THE MACHINE
Courtesy of Epic Records
By arrangement with Sony Music Licensing

'RELOAD'
Written by ROB ZOMBIE and SCOTT HUMPHREY
Produced by SCOTT HUMPHREY and ROB ZOMBIE
Remixed by CHARLIE CLOUSER
Performed by ROB ZOMBIE

Courtesy of Geffen Records
Under licence from Universal Music Enterprises

'SLEEPING AWAKE'
Written by P.O.D.
Produced by HOWARD BENSON
Mixed by CHRIS LORD-ALGE
Performed by P.O.D.
Courtesy of Atlantic Recording Corp.
By arrangement with Warner Strategic Marketing

'SESSION'
Written by LINKIN PARK
Produced by DON GILMORE and LINKIN PARK
Performed by LINKIN PARK
Courtesy of Warner Bros. Records Inc.
By Arrangement with Warner Strategic Marketing

'WHEN THE WORLD ENDS (OAKENFOLD REMIX)'
Written by DAVID J. MATTHEWS and GLEN BALLARD
Produced by GLEN BALLARD
Performed by DAVE MATTHEWS BAND
Courtesy of The RCA Records Label, a unit of BMG Music
Under licence from BMG Special Products

Filmed at FOX STUDIOS, AUSTRALIA
Sydney and Alameda, California
This Motion Picture © 2003 Warner Bros. Entertainment Inc.
US, Canada, Bahamas & Bermuda
© 2003 Village Roadshow Films (BVI) Limited
All Other Territories

100
100
100
001
000
101
010
100
110
100
001
100
100
101
000
010
100
001
011
000
010
110
101
000
101
011
101
001
001
010
101
010
101
001
001
011
001
001
000
010
001
010
101
001
101
000

About the Author

Paul Condon was born in Liverpool in 1970 and spent far too long reading and being a swot at school, which more or less explains why he's so obsessed with movies, TV and pop culture. Paul graduated from Nottingham University with a degree in English and has worked in conference management, recruitment, marketing and most recently running celebrity web-chats for the BBC. He has co-written a book on the movies of Alfred Hitchcock for Virgin Books, and regularly contributes articles for *Film Review*, *Starburst* and *TV Zone*. *Six Feet Under: The Unofficial Guide*, his first solo book, is published by Contender Books.

24: The Unofficial Guide

Jim Sangster
£7.99 / Paperback / Published July 2002
ISBN 1 84357 034 3

'Right now, terrorists are plotting to assassinate a presidential candidate, my wife and daughter are in danger and people that I work with may be involved in both.'

A day that begins with simple family trouble soon becomes the longest day ever for Federal Agent Jack Bauer, after Jack is alerted to a possible assassination attempt on Presidential Candidate David Palmer. As the plot thickens and the web of conspiracy widens, the seconds keep ticking away...

This is the unofficial guide to *24*, the hit espionage thriller starring Emmy Award winner Kiefer Sutherland, where each episode marks another hour of real-time drama. With a detailed breakdown of the events as they unfold – the shocks, the surprises and the many twists and turns – it's the essential companion to the most captivating, 'must-see' drama on TV.

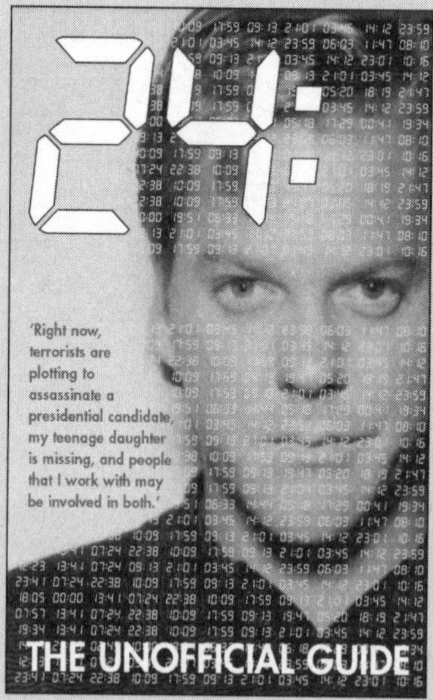

24: Season 2 – The Unofficial Guide

Mark Wright
£7.99 / Paperback / Published July 2003
ISBN 1 84357 072 6

24, the most talked-about show of 2002 returns for a second day in the life of Federal Agent Jack Bauer, played by Golden Globe winning actor Kiefer Sutherland. Watching the tragic events of Season One unfold in real-time action, it seemed that things couldn't get any worse. But, tomorrow is always another day…

Set 18 months after the first, award winning season, Jack has left CTU and is still coming to terms with the death of his wife. However, the now President Palmer recalls Jack to help CTU he is the only man who can prevent a terrorist plot to detonate a nuclear bomb in Los Angeles in the next 24 hours. With his daughter Kim missing and unable to trust anyone, the race is on to prevent the beginning of World War III. But time is running out…

24: Season 2: The Unofficial Guide contains everything you need to know about the critically acclaimed second season of the hottest show on TV. With mission briefs, detailed episode breakdowns, profiles of the cast and crew and full reviews for every hour, this is the only guide to take you through the action minute by minute.

Tick, tick, tick…

Andromeda – The High Guard Handbook

Gareth Wigmore & Thomasina Gibson
£12.99 / Paperback / Published May 2003
ISBN 1 84357 033 5

Set in deep, deep space, Gene Roddenberry's Andromeda chronicles the adventures of Captain Dylan Hunt and his motley crew of humans, super-humans, aliens and AI's as they fight to restore peace and posterity to a fractured universe.

Debuting as the highest rated SF show in syndication, the Gemini Award-winning Andromeda continues to scale the heights of television excellence all over the globe with superb writing, a supreme case and superlative visual effects.

The High Guard Handbook is an indispensable bible for *Andromeda* fans. Contained within its pages are the most definitive episode guides ever written for the show, giving detailed plot information for each of the episodes in the first two seasons. This fully illustrated book also includes race histories and character biographies, in-depth character guides and exclusive interviews with the cast and crew.

ER: The Unofficial Guide

Mark Jones
£9.99 / Paperback / Pubished February 2003
ISBN 1 84357 035 1

ER – The Unofficial Guide covers the first eight series of the award winning medical drama that has kept viewers gripped for nearly a decade. This illustrated book is packed full of detail on each episode and charts every character from Carter's early student days to Carol Hathaway and Doug Ross's rocky relationship and Mark Green's tragic illness.

ER – The Unofficial Guide also contains season overviews, colour pictures, cast biographies and special features on the best episodes from each series. An indispensable guide for the true ER enthusiast.

Six Feet Under: The Unofficial Guide

Paul Condon
£7.99 / Paperback / Published October 2002
ISBN 1 84357 037 8

This is the story of the Fishers, a family of Funeral Directors trying to make sense of life and death in the City of Angels. With more sex, swearing and genuine irony than you'd expect from an American TV show, the Golden Globe award-winning *Six Feet Under*, created and co-written by Oscar winner Alan Ball, is one of the most talked about programmes this side of Heaven or Hell.

This unofficial guide to the first two seasons of *Six Feet Under* selects the highlights of each episode and offers a handy route-planner to the Afterlife. Detailing the funniest (and most poignant) moments, cast and crew biographies, soundtrack references, and a complete listing of every corpse to grace the Fisher & Sons slab, *Six Feet Under: The Unofficial Guide* is an indispensable handbook to this original and innovative drama.

Spooks Confidential: The Official Handbook

Jim Sangster
£9.99 / Paperback / Published August 2003
ISBN 1 84357 069 6

MI5, not 9 to 5.

Take a look inside MI5, the intelligence agency in charge of defending the UK's domestic security. Every day, these people investigate and assess threats posed to Britain by terrorists, enemies of the state and international organised crime, using intelligence and the latest in technology to counter Britain's enemies at every step.

To some, they're known as spies. To us, they're SPOOKS.

This access-all-areas book features exclusive interviews with the cast and production crews and top-secret insider information on the making of the series, as well as character biogs an episode-by-episode breakdown for both series and a guide to BBCi's internet-based interactive episode. With background analysis of the show's plot points, a history of MI5 and examinations of the real-life issues behind the storylines, [spooks] Confidential allows you to enter the world of secrets, intrigue and treachery with full insider knowledge.